The Way of Lovingkindness

AN IMPERFECT PROCESS OF
SPIRITUAL ENGAGEMENT

The Way of Lovingkindness

David Orendorff

The Way of Lovingkindness: An Imperfect Process of Spiritual Engagement
© 2021 David Orendorff

Paperback ISBN: 979-8-218-07801-0
Ebook ISBN: 979-8-218-07802-7

Cover design by Emily Mahon
Interior design by Liz Schreiter
Edited and produced by Reading List Editorial
ReadingListEditorial.com

I write this book for my wife, Vickie, who embodies lovingkindness.

I write this book for my children, Erika, Johanna, and Priya, who teach me lovingkindness.

I write this book for my grandchildren, Ashlyn, Addisen, Thea, and Trey, that they may know and live lovingkindness.

I write this book for any who need to be reminded that they are loved.

Lovingkindness desired to be
and so breathed life into time and space.

The Cosmos was born.

We are the body
of Lovingkindness.

CONTENTS

Preface

The contents of this book have been used and revised for classes and workshops over four decades. It is both a memoir and a defining of my spiritual journey. It reflects the wisdom of the community in which I have traveled. What I write is a snapshot of my life in process. I pray to continue growing in lovingkindness.

The art within the book was created by my grandson, Trey Schaaf. Trey began making art as a child. Creativity is his therapy and haven from abuse. Each of Trey's creations for this book are responses to specific concepts of the book and have been strategically placed by him.

A warning to the reader: I don't know what I am talking about. I don't know the absolute truth. I am not being humble; I don't think any of us knows absolute truth. We are like those in Plato's cave, who can only guess at the meaning and purpose of the shadows on the wall. We can only give our best thoughts based upon our own experiences, understandings, and studies.

A confession to the reader: The fundamental principle of this book is "God is Lovingkindness." Logically it follows that Lovingkindness is God. For me, God and lovingkindness are interchangeable. My imperfect efforts to serve God are manifest in my imperfect efforts to serve lovingkindness. I am not the model of lovingkindness, though I intend and strive to practice what I preach. Sometimes I succeed. Sometimes I fail.

It will be important for the reader to understand that, for me, creation is not inert matter that can be disassembled into ever smaller mechanical parts. Creation is a single living organism composed of energy and matter, experienced in time and space, that regulates itself for the existence of life. For Earth, our biosphere, this understanding has been proposed as the Gaia hypothesis. Inger Andersen, the executive director of the United Nations Environment Programme, is quoted by Richard Grossman as saying, "The Gaia hypothesis holds that all living and non-living components on Earth work together to sustain life by homeostatic mechanisms. It proposes that organisms, and their inorganic surroundings on Earth, are closely integrated to form a single, self-regulating complex system, maintaining the conditions necessary for life."[1] I extend this hypothesis to include the whole of the cosmos, all of creation. Without stars manufacturing the elements of life, life does not exist. Consequently, humans are not detached observers of creation but members of the cosmic organism, just as cells are members of the human body. And just as the body, from cell to organ to person, has a unified purpose for the well-being of the whole, so too does creation. When I speak of lovingkindness acting for the well-being of creation, I am speaking of the creation as one cosmic organism, from quantum to galaxy, from quark to human. I recommend Edward Goldsmith's *The Way: An Ecological World-View* as an excellent source to explore creation as a single organism having a unified purpose. I name the purpose of creation to be lovingkindness.

Some have asked me, "Why do you define Greek words so often?" Greek is the language of Christian scripture (also called the New Testament), and Christian scripture is primary to my spiritual understanding. Researching the original Greek text clarifies what the words attempt to convey in a way that reading another's translation may not. The Greek words are as close as I can come to hearing the words of Jesus and Paul, and those are the words I want to hear.

Not all Christians have the same understanding of Hebrew and Christian scripture, the Bible. To avoid confusion and misunderstanding I offer my view. In a culture that wants right answers, offering a process without answers, as I do, is challenging. Culturally we want the

---

1   Richard Grossman, "Consider the Gaia Hypothesis," *MAHB Blog*, Millennium Alliance for Humanity and the Biosphere, September 15, 2020, https://mahb.stanford.edu/blog/consider-the-gaia-hypothesis/.

right formula, the right recipe, the right instruction manual, and an assured result. The Bible is subsequently treated as a science, history, law, or self-help book. For me the Bible is the family story of encounters with God over time. Sometimes our family story is spot-on. Sometimes, not so much. But behind every book and passage of the Bible is the search for wisdom within the folly of being God's people. The Bible tells the story and process of becoming the creation God desires. The Bible tells us from whence we came, signals wrong turns, and offers the possibilities of where we might go.

I am a United Methodist. Methodists received their name from being methodical about their spiritual practices. Being a Methodist by heritage and at heart, I have organized the practice of lovingkindness into a method or system. My thoughts might be mental tricks, rationalizations, or wishful thinking, and the value of my practices might be a self-fulfilling expectation. Such is the human condition.

Foolishly I attempt to organize the Spirit. However, the Gospel of John says, "The wind (Spirit) blows where it wills, and you hear the sound of it, but you do not know from where it comes or to where it goes; so it is with everyone who is born of the Spirit."[2] In my experience John is right. Yet knowing I fail to capture the wind, I persist.

In ignominious hubris, I attempt to systematize the practical theology and method of John Wesley, a primary founder of Methodism. My systematic presentation of John Wesley's theology is not from him. Like the Apostle Paul, John Wesley was a practical theologian. He wrote his notes and sermons to the lives of people as they were being lived. He did not write a systematic or apologetic theological treatise. Wesley does not offer a well-tied shoelace. The system is my imposition. To be clear, this essay is my belief system viewed through a scratched Wesleyan lens.

---

2   John 3:8. Quoted scripture is my translation using the Greek text of *Deutsche Bibelgesellschaft* (Stuttgart, 1979), as printed in the *Nestle-Aland Greek-English New Testament,* (2nd ed., 1985) or the Hebrew text of the *Hebrew-English TANAKH,* (Philadelphia: The Jewish Publication Society, 2nd ed.,1999).

I write of a spiritual path that is a method or process and not a creed or dogma. The United Methodist Church is something of an anomaly among Christian congregations in that it does not require loyalty to any creed. When asked, "What do you believe as a Methodist?" many a United Methodist is stymied. The answer I give is "I believe in a method, a process, a way of lovingkindness." The way of lovingkindness does not offer a catechism of beliefs but a process of spiritual engagement. When I am at my best, I am not concerned with being right or correct. My best self is concerned with being in relationship with God and others so that together we are transformed toward a lovingkindness that seeks the well-being of all. I want less often to argue to be right and more often to listen for learning, understanding, and mutual spiritual growth. I want less often to judge and more often to grow in humble lovingkindness.

Because God creates and loves diversity in all things, I have also learned the way of lovingkindness from sources other than United Methodism, Christianity, and Judaism. Valued teachers outside my faith tradition are the depth psychologist Carl Jung, the spiritual and social activist Mahatma Gandhi, the philosophical and religious book *Tao Te Ching*, and the beliefs and practices of Mahayana and Zen Buddhism. Quantum physics, in which bundles of energy wonderfully become hydrogen, helium, stars, elements, and biomatter, is another teacher of lovingkindness. I have many teachers, but what I desire to convey is that the path I outline is not the one right way. It is my hope that what I offer displays essential characteristics of any path that would transform us into a loving people who heal creation. What I am certain of is that lovingkindness makes my being alive quite wonderful. So wonderful that I recommend lovingkindness to you.

Introduction

For forty-seven years, I have been a pastor in the United Methodist Church. Though I officially retired in 2014, I continue to be a pastor. I am a pastor more by accident than by intention. I had no idea I would be who I have become. My first career choice, made in the fifth grade, was to be an attorney. In the sixth grade it was to be an astronaut. When I learned that wearing glasses prohibited me from being either a pilot or an astronaut, I moved my aspirations to becoming an aeronautical engineer. For several years I stuck with engineering. In the fall of 1967, I entered Northwest Community College in Powell, Wyoming, as an engineering student. Then everything changed.

My first year of college I went exploring. I experimented with alcohol, marijuana, LSD, a little hash, and some speed. My parents, with whom I lived, became disgusted with me. It was understandable, since I was dealing drugs out of their house. When I said, at the beginning of the summer of 1968, that I wanted to hitchhike from Powell to Casper, Wyoming, to look for work, my mother helped me pack a suitcase and drove me to the edge of town, where she gladly left me. In Casper, I picked up Rick, a high school friend, and we hitchhiked to Denver. There I smoked some dope and worked as a door-to-door encyclopedia salesman. It was the summer of Denver's racial protests, and our apartment was in the middle of the violence and anger. I became a firm supporter of racial justice, and I had my first mystical experience. I decided I wanted to live and love like Jesus. You will learn the details later.

I quit my encyclopedia job and hitchhiked to a "religious" commune in Estes Park, Colorado. It was a scam. Little Jesus, the self-identified spiritual leader of the commune, stole a kid's sleeping bag and fled with his sidekick, John the Baptist, to a peyote festival in the desert Southwest. An ex–Hell's Angel girl bit my hand, and I got extremely ill, had unmentionable gastric issues, lost significant weight, and hitchhiked home to Powell, where I was diagnosed with hepatitis A.

In September of 1968, I returned to college. I took a part-time job as a youth pastor at the local United Methodist Church. I began a two-year process of becoming drug-free. I attempted to change my major to drama and English. My math and physics professors argued with me because I was one of their top students. They reported me to my father, who was the college president. He argued with me. I earned an associate's degree in science with an unusual amount of drama and English credits. The first semester of my junior year was at the University of Wyoming. The classes were too big for my liking, and the friendships too shallow. In January of 1970, I transferred to Rocky Mountain College in Billings, Montana. There I met and dated Vickie Egeland. After I graduated in the summer of 1971 with a bachelor's degree, having majored in math, sociology, English, and drama, Vickie and I were married. Vickie is the full love of my life, and she repeatedly appears when I think and write on the nature of love. Vickie grew up in the small town of Big Timber, Montana, within a very loving family. She embodies lovingkindness without having to conceptualize or discuss it. She intuits what is needed and then does it. After I spontaneously blurted out a marriage proposal and she agreed, I returned to my dorm room. I was full of fear, uncertainty, and questions about what I had just done. I didn't know my future. I had no steady income. There was no plan beyond loving Vickie. I prayed, "Dear God, help me." A strong image came over me. It was the feel and sound of cosmic laughter and a voice spoke inside my head: "Aha, I got you." It was my second experience of the mystical.

In January of 1972, I began attending the Methodist Theological School in Ohio. It was not my intention to become a pastor. I didn't know what I wanted to do, but I liked school, was pretty good at it, and was curious about the Bible and theology. During the four years of seminary, I was both a student and a youth pastor. I graduated with a master's in divinity, the standard seminary degree, and a master's in Christianity and drama, which focused on the history of Christian drama and producing drama in the local church. I still didn't want to be a pastor, and so I applied to various graduate schools for PhD programs in the New Testament. Of the schools that accepted me, I chose Claremont Graduate School, east of Los Angeles.

At Claremont I was again both a student and a youth pastor. I completed all the requirements for the PhD—classes, languages, competency exams. My dissertation on Jesus' miraculous feedings was three-quarters done and approved. Then Vickie and I decided to have children. Children meant Vickie would not be working. That meant I needed a real job. I had limited alternatives. I decided to be a pastor. Being a youth pastor had been positive, the church would pay me money, and I could finish my dissertation while serving a congregation. I chose United Methodism because of my family and seminary history. We chose Montana because we wanted to be close to our families.

In September of 1975, Vickie and I moved with our three-month-old baby from the LA area, population 7.5 million, to Sunburst, Montana, population 450. I was to serve the small United Methodist congregations of Sunburst, Kevin, and Sweetgrass. When we arrived, word immediately spread, and the good folk of Sunburst quickly came to meet us and help us unload the U-Haul that contained, besides the usual stuff, a sixteen-foot catamaran sailboat, five cases of wine, and twenty or so boxes of books. In my defense, the wine was mostly the fulfillment of a request from Vickie's family. To complete the picture, my hair was long, and I was dressed Southern Cal informal in a muscle shirt and cutoffs. Despite the contents of the U-Haul and my appearance, the folks accepted and loved us, mostly, I think, because of Vickie and the baby.

The first year in Sunburst, I learned that no Montana library had the resources I needed to complete my dissertation, not even the university libraries. It was a time before the luxury of computers and the internet. Without luck, I struggled to get resources by mail. After two years the dissertation was abandoned without regret. I discovered I loved being a pastor and I didn't need the PhD for my career or ego. In 1978 I was ordained as a United Methodist pastor. We spent four great years with the people of North Toole County, had a second daughter, and were sad when my bishop directed us to move to Polson, Montana, to pastor the United Methodist Church there.

After four years in Polson, we were appointed to St. Paul's United Methodist Church in Helena, Montana. It was at St. Paul's in 1988 that I developed and began to regularly teach a class about the healing power of God's love. I called the class Amazing Grace. It became a staple for the remainder of my ministry. The class evolved over time because of conversations with the participants, new material, and my ongoing transformation. Several class members have requested that I turn the class into a book. I resisted because since it was difficult for me to write a sermon weekly, how could I ever write a book?

In June of 2020 I was diagnosed with advanced metastatic prostate cancer. Fortunately, the hormone therapy I am on is lengthening my life. Cancer convinced me that I am finite. I decided to write the Amazing Grace class into this book for all those who asked and for my children and grandchildren, who call me Pop. I want them to have a record of my life and faith, and perhaps find something useful for their lives.

What I write is a way of life, a spiritual system, built on understanding the fundamental force of life to be lovingkindness. This way of life is lived in gratitude for creation, acceptance of forgiveness, and simple practices that offer cooperation with the Spirit. I frame this way of life in my Christian and United Methodist tradition. However, it is not my desire that you be Christian or United Methodist. It is my desire that beneath my story and my tradition you discover your own connection to lovingkindness and perhaps a deeper life of well-being as an individual, in community, and for the Earth. It is my prayer that what I write can help some of us more often be the lovingkindness we are made to be, and thereby be healers of creation.

Two Kinds of Salvation

The current formative narrative of salvation for much of Western Christianity evolved from the debt-satisfaction and penal-substitution theories, which became predominate in the European feudal and monarchical culture of the eleventh to thirteenth centuries. I name what has evolved "punitive salvation." In punitive salvation, God is the king who writes the rules, convenes the court, is the jury, and enforces the necessary punishment. Jesus, the son of the king God and therefore the prince, saves the rebellious people from king God's punishment by substituting his death for theirs, thus rescuing the people from eternal prison.

Christian evangelists from the punitive salvation school sometimes ask, "Are you saved?" For them, being saved means you are going to Heaven and not to Hell. Being saved requires admitting to being a sinner and accepting Jesus as your savior. Punitive salvation offers both a carrot and a stick. The carrot is the promise of eternal paradise. The stick is the threat of eternal damnation.

What follows is the theory of punitive salvation offered in story form. A friend emailed it to me. The author was not identified, so I am unable to give credit. It is a good description of the fundamentals of punitive salvation.

> After living what I felt was a decent life, my time on earth came to its end. The first thing I remember is sitting on a bench in the waiting room of what I thought to be a courthouse. The doors opened and I was instructed to come in and have a seat

by the defense table. As I entered, I saw the prosecutor. He was villainous looking and maniacally grinned at me. I sat down where I was instructed and looked to my left. There sat my attorney, a kind and gentle looking man whose appearance seemed so familiar to me. I felt I knew him.

The corner door flew open and there appeared the Judge in full flowing robes. He commanded an awesome presence as He moved across the room. I couldn't take my eyes off Him. As He took His seat behind the bench, He said, "Let us begin."

The prosecutor rose and said, "Your Honor, my name is Satan, and I am here to show you why this man belongs in Hell." He proceeded to tell of lies I told, things I stole, when I cheated, when my words and my violence wounded. Satan told of other horrible perversions that had been in my life and the more he spoke, the further down in my seat I sank.

I was so embarrassed and ashamed that I couldn't look at anyone, not even my own Attorney. The Devil told of sins I had completely forgotten. As upset as I was at Satan for telling all these things about me, I was equally upset with my attorney, who silently sat there, not offering any form of defense, for not all my life had been so ugly.

I know I had been guilty of those things, but I had done some good in my life—couldn't that at least equal out part of the harm I'd done? Satan finished with a fury and said, "This man belongs in Hell; he is guilty of all that I have charged and there is not a person who can prove otherwise."

When it was His turn, My Attorney first asked if He might approach the bench. The Judge allowed this over the strong objection of Satan and beckoned Him to come forward. As He got up and started walking, I was able to see Him in His full splendor and majesty. I realized why He seemed so familiar; this was Jesus representing me, my Lord and my Savior.

He stopped at the bench and softly said to the Judge, "Hi, Dad," and then He turned to address the court. "Satan was correct in saying that this man had sinned; I won't deny any of these allegations. And, yes, the wages of sin is death, and this man deserves to be punished." Jesus took a deep breath and turned to His Father with outstretched arms and proclaimed, "However, I died on the cross so that this person might have eternal life and he has accepted Me as his Savior, so he is Mine."

My Lord continued with, "His name is written in the Book of Life, and no one can snatch him from me. Satan does not yet understand. This man is not to be given justice, but rather mercy." As Jesus sat down, He quietly paused, looked at His Father and said, "There is nothing else that needs to be done. I've done it all."

The Judge lifted His mighty hand and slammed the gavel down. The following words bellowed from His lips. "This man is free. The penalty for him has already been paid in full. Case dismissed."

As my Lord led me away, I could hear Satan ranting and raving. "I won't give up. I will win the next one." I asked Jesus, as He gave me my instructions where to go next, "Have you ever lost a case?" Christ lovingly smiled and said, "Everyone that has come to Me and asked Me to represent them has received the same verdict as you: paid in full."

The story describes how many understand God, humans, and salvation. God has decreed laws. We have broken the laws. We must be punished. Jesus substitutes himself for our punishment by being crucified for our sins and going to Hell in our place. God accepts Jesus' substitution by removing Jesus from Hell, raising him from the dead, and forgiving us. However, only those who accept Jesus as Lord can escape the eternal suffering of Hell. Punitive salvation has deep roots in our culture and the human psyche. The hierarchical, legalistic, and punishing message of punitive salvation is expressed explicitly and implicitly not only in our churches but also in our personal relationships, in how we parent, and in our educational, judicial, and political systems. There are rules, and those who break the rules must be punished unless a substitute can be offered.

I challenge this view of God as king and Jesus as substitutionary prince. I offer a primary understanding of God as lovingkindness, servant, and healer. I and others call this the theory of therapeutic salvation. Therapeutic salvation originates with Jesus' earliest followers and offers a way to reconciliation with God, people, and all creation. When Jesus is said to heal someone, the Greek word most used in Christian scripture is *therapeuo*—in English, to give therapy, to care for, to heal.[1] The root of the word "salvation" is "salve," a healing balm. Jesus' way of salvation is a healing balm for creation—hence therapeutic salvation.

When Jesus asked his disciples to follow him, his call is translated into the Greek word *akoloutheo*, which has the connotation of imitation. The earliest followers of Jesus sought to imitate Jesus' way of healing love. The earliest understanding of being a follower of Jesus was to live and love like Jesus. The primary focus of therapeutic salvation is on imitating Jesus by trusting God and by healing individuals, communities, and the creation through relationships built upon lovingkindness. Therapeutic salvation heals this life by imitating Jesus' faith in God and his lovingkindness for the well-being of all.

Paul, the earliest writer of Christian scripture, supports the imitation of Jesus in his letter to the churches in Rome and Galatia. The usual translation of what Paul writes is "(humans are made right with God) through faith *in* Jesus Christ."[2] This translation is based on punitive salvation's understanding of Jesus as substitute with the requirement to accept Jesus' lordship, to have faith in Jesus Christ. The same Greek phrase can also be translated as "(humans are made right with

---

1   The definitions of Greek words are taken from *A Greek-English Lexicon*, compiled by Henry George Liddell and Robert Scott (Oxford: Clarendon Press, 1968 edition), or *A Lexicon, Abridged from Liddell and Scott's Greek-English Lexicon* (New York, Chicago, Cincinnati: American Book Company, 1909 edition).

2   Romans 3:22; Galatians 2:16.

God) through the faith of Jesus Christ." The shift of the preposition from *in* to *of* shifts the focus from Jesus as the one who substitutes for humanity to Jesus as the one who models faith for humanity.

Below is a foundational story of therapeutic salvation as I would tell it.

My job is challenging, and I think it is helpful in making a better world. I am glad to be the team leader. My work team is terrific. Or it was terrific until I made an arrogant error. We had a team opening, and I invited a friend to apply. I thought she would be a great addition and I was insistent that she be hired even though the personnel department had doubts. For two years things went well. Then there were problems. Our formerly outstanding team was performing poorly and was increasingly having interpersonal disputes. The problems became serious dysfunction, and our customers began to suffer.

After consulting with our supervisor, the team invited a group therapist to meet with us monthly for a year. As we isolated the issues it became clear that the primary problem was the working relationship between my friend and me. We were sabotaging each other in subtle ways, and our covert conflict was bleeding into the rest of the team. The team and our customers needed us to find healthy ways to work together.

To make a long story short, my now ex-friend and I met with the therapist for another year. We had no success; in fact, things got worse. Relationships were strained, productivity continued to decline, and the team members began to take sides. Our service and sales were declining, and we were losing longtime customers.

The two years of struggle were some of the longest and most difficult years of my life. I doubted my value to the team, our customers, and the world. I became depressed, started antidepressant medication, and had private therapy.

My relationships with my wife and children were increasingly strained. I grieved the loss of not only my friend, but also other friends, as lines were drawn, and sides were taken. I functioned minimally during the day and slept poorly at night. I needed help.

A pastor friend suggested I go on a seven-day silent retreat at a Benedictine retreat center. The thought of going for a week without talking to anyone but a spiritual director once a day frightened me. I was afraid of what she would discover about me. I was afraid of what I might discover about me. I was afraid of the silence. I went anyway because I was more afraid of my growing insanity.

At the retreat my spiritual director forbade me to read and instructed me to spend my time outdoors, simply observing. I took long walks through the surrounding woods or sat and looked at the life around me. I was sitting and contemplating a grotto dedicated to Mother Mary when into my head sprang the lyrics to the Beatles' "Let It Be." I know the lyrics were written about the mother of Paul McCartney. Though she had died when he was fourteen, he found she still came to him "in times of trouble." However, I heard "Let It Be" as words of wisdom from Mary, the mother of Jesus. I let go of what I wanted and listened for what God wanted. The retreat revived my spirit, and I was able to be both more direct and kinder with the team and more loving to my family.

Six months later I again went on a seven-day silent retreat at the Benedictine center. Sitting on a small bench overlooking a green valley I felt a still, small voice urge, "Tell your supervisor that one of you needs to be moved." I responded, "Who will be moved?" The voice answered, "That depends on many decisions that others must make." I wanted assurance that I would stay. It was my team. I had given it sixteen years of my life. But the voice offered no assurances. I trusted the voice, wrote the letter to my supervisor, and was confident that no matter who was moved, I would be at peace. My contact with the love of God deepened, and my peace in the situation and with life became more solid. My spiritual director gave me Psalm 131 as a daily mantra:

> YHWH, my heart has no lofty ambitions,
> my eyes do not look too high.
> I am not concerned with great affairs,
> or marvels beyond my scope.
> Enough for me to keep my soul tranquil and quiet,
> like a child in its mother's arms,
> as content as a child that has been weaned.
> People of God, rely on YHWH, now and for always.

I was hurt that my supervisor chose to move me. But I trusted the direction of the Spirit. My new team in a new state renewed me. Our work together was productive, useful to many, peaceful, and joyful. I loved my new town, where I became active in a service club and sailing. My wife was diagnosed with breast cancer and our new location had the medical team she needed. The move may have saved her life.

As my need to be successful and right diminished and my trust in the Spirit grew, I more often thought and acted in lovingkindness. Though I was sad to leave my old team and our customers, my new life was and is a blessing, a gift of the Spirit. As dark as those days were, they were also the days that laid the foundation for the greatness of the following twenty years.

I grew up being taught the story of punitive salvation. It is the story of therapeutic salvation that now guides and shapes me. Therapeutic salvation teaches that I need not fear God nor wait for death to know the lovingkindness of God. Its emphasis on compassion and well-being in this life inspires me and directs me, offering guidance and healing for the struggles of today, bringing peace amid turmoil and hope in times of despair.

Punitive salvation is fear based. It threatens rejection by God and God's people. It threatens punishment if we don't keep God's laws. It threatens eternal damnation and torture, an assignment to Hell, if we don't meet its criteria. Therapeutic salvation is based in lovingkindness. It is an invitation to belong to God, to each other, and to creation with gratitude, forgiveness, and healing. It is the way of life that seeks the well-being of all. John, in his first letter to the churches, calls out fear-based religion when he writes, "There is no fear in lovingkindness, but complete lovingkindness casts out fear. For fear has to do with punishment, and whoever fears is not complete in lovingkindness."[3]

Punitive salvation has at its heart a corruption of the original intention of the laws of Moses, which are also called the Torah. Moses' laws are offered as a way of life that produces fruitful and peaceful relationships with God, our neighbors, and ourselves. Some of the laws may seem silly, parochial, cruel, or arcane to us, but their original intent was to guide us toward living safely with each other. Punitive salvation fails when it turns guidance into requirements for God's approval and threatens those who do not keep these requirements with eternal damnation. Therapeutic salvation restores the original purpose of law as guidance. In therapeutic salvation, God is the great therapist and physician who creates life, makes house calls, offers guidance, and gives well-being. When we fail to be lovingkindness, the therapeutic God forgives us and offers us a renewed opportunity to live in lovingkindness.

Law points a direction for the well-being of all. Without the guidance of law, therapeutic salvation becomes chaos, and law without lovingkindness becomes cruel. Law reminds us that there is suffering when we fail to be lovingkindness. It condemns but does not heal. Therapeutic salvation reminds us that there is forgiveness and reconciliation. Both law and love are necessary, but neither is complete in

---

3   1 John 4:18.

and of itself. Jesus said, "Do not think that I have come to abolish the law or the prophets: I have come not to abolish but to fulfill them."[4] Therapeutic salvation is the fulfillment of the intention of the law and the intention of the prophets to heal what is broken among us. The law, when rightly read, points to healing lovingkindness as the way we might live in well-being and justice. Without the law, we have no guidelines. Without lovingkindness, we have no purpose and no mercy.

When I first attended Alcoholics Anonymous, I needed both law and love. At my first AA meeting, I was given specific instructions for a path to sobriety and serenity. I was told, "Go to sixty meetings in sixty days. Read the Big Book. Get a sponsor. Work the twelve steps." If at my first meeting I was simply told, "Feel the love," I would still be a drunk. In the early days of sobriety, I needed specific, actionable, and measurable goals. Only later in the process do many of us discover the freedom those AA rules have given us in living our lives.

Punitive salvation argues that Jesus' death is a substitute for the punishment we deserve. The punitive God can only have justice if someone is punished for breaking divine law. The salvation gained for us by Jesus substituting for us is called substitutionary atonement. Therapeutic salvation is not based on substitutionary atonement, but on forgiveness. Jesus prayed from the cross, "Abba, forgive them, for they do not know what they are doing."[5] *Abba* is Hebrew and Aramaic for "father" or "daddy." Jesus was not bargaining with his daddy to be a substitute for us; he was praying to Abba to have mercy on us, to forgive us.[6]

In his first letter to the churches, John writes, "Jesus is the expiation for our sins, and not for ours only but also for the sins of the whole cosmos"[7] and "In this is love, not that we loved God, but that God loved us and sent his Son to be the expiation for our sins."[8] These

---

4   Matthew 5:17.

5   Luke 23:34.

6   For a biblical and process theological presentation of God as Jesus' Abba, see John Cobb's *Jesus' Abba: The God who Has Not Failed* (Minneapolis: Fortress Press, 2015).

7   1 John 2:2.

8   1 John 4:10.

two passages are often used to promote the theory of substitutionary atonement. The Greek word translated as expiation is *hilasmos*. It is also sometimes translated as "atoning sacrifice." Hilasmos is an action meant to repair a relationship that has been injured or broken. Some Christians understand hilasmos to mean substitutionary atonement.

Suppose I said something to Vickie that betrayed our love. An hilasmos can be my apology that seeks forgiveness. But my apology might not be enough to heal what I have broken. I may need to do something like sleep on the couch, an atoning sacrifice. Substitutionary atonement would be for Vickie to make a grandchild sleep on the couch because of my sin. I don't see that happening. Ultimately, no matter the hilasmos I may offer, it is Vickie who restores our relationship by forgiving me for failing our love. Likewise, God, independent of whatever action I may take, reconciles our relationship by graciously forgiving me, thus healing what I have broken. I am the one that fails; Vickie and God are the ones who set aside my failure with their forgiving love. In therapeutic salvation, God freely forgives us when Jesus asks Abba to forgive us. It is God who restores our relationship because God chooses to do so.

Punitive salvation is often used to blame those who suffer for their pain. We are blamed for our broken lives and said to be deserving of eternal damnation. The abused spouse is told they must have done something to enrage their partner and are therefore being punished. The abused child is told their misbehavior brings the wrath of parents as godly justice. The ill are told their disease is God's wrath or their failed faith. The poor are told that their poverty is their failure and God's punishment. People of color, those of differing sexuality, and migrants have all been blamed and punished in the name of the punitive God. Believing that our suffering is God's punishment, we are led to the question, "What did I do to piss God off?"

In therapeutic salvation, our suffering is not a punishment from God. God wants our well-being, not our torture. It is true that sometimes we inflict our own wounds, suffering the consequences of our own actions. Often, we suffer the consequences of the failings of another, or of a society, or of the simple fragility of being alive. Sometimes the guiltiest are left unpunished. In therapeutic salvation, suffering and injustice are acknowledged as conditions inherent to being alive, and God is viewed as the heavenly power who loves us and will assist us to endure, if not end, suffering.

Built into punitive salvation is a hierarchy of power that has been used to empower some and oppress others. God, the powerful king at the top, distributes power to chosen persons, who then distribute power to their chosen, and so on down to the powerless. In Western culture, based on this hierarchical model from punitive Christianity, the male descendants of Europe are lifted above all others. This is particularly true in how the punitive God has been used to justify and promote the ravages of colonialism through the concepts of manifest destiny, the doctrine of discovery, and the white man's burden to civilize the world. I am a white, educated, cisgender, heterosexual, middle-class male. For centuries in Western culture, those like me have been given authority to decide who is in and who is out, who is right and who is wrong, who is rich and who is poor, who is in prison and who escapes judgment, who is sane and who is crazy, who is worthy of support and who can starve. I, and those like me, have defined who can vote, who can do what jobs at what pay, who has access to quality education, who can own homes and where, and who can be lynched. For centuries, white men like me have claimed that our power over others is God-given. Until quite recently, God has often been portrayed as a white male, even in non-white churches and cultures. It disturbs some when God is portrayed as a woman or a person of color. Our Western culture is built around a hierarchy of white male feudal lords claiming power to reward or punish. Women, children, people of color, indigenous peoples, people of the LGBTQ+ community, people with challenging conditions, the poor, and people unlike me are strung out toward the bottom of power and privilege. I am their judge and systemically, if not personally, their executioner. Those like me are historically and currently the privileged chosen of punitive salvation.

In therapeutic salvation, God is the healer of the wounded. There are no chosen or preferred groups, heritages, genders, sects, or heirs. Those with power are to use it to support the powerless in their struggle for well-being. Those with wealth are to use it to support the poor in their efforts for well-being. Those with privilege are to use it to support the oppressed in their fight for well-being. Those with knowledge are to use it to support the well-being of all. The therapeutic God of lovingkindness serves the well-being of the whole of creation.

The God of punitive salvation is ultimately impotent. This king can threaten us with punishment for our failures, for the insane chaos and suffering we create, but threats, no matter how divine or eternal, have not and cannot save us from self-destruction. Punitive salvation condemns us, but it does not save us, it does not heal us, and it does not give us abundant life. Therapeutic salvation judges but does not condemn. It judges what heals and what wounds. It forgives those who wound and offers to them and their victims healing and a future of well-being.

Some might ask, "Therapeutic salvation is a good thought for this life, but what happens to me in the next life?" We have been conditioned to ask this question by the eight-hundred-year dominance of the punitive model of salvation. In punitive salvation, God's healing of broken situations and lives is canceled with our last breath. Suddenly, at death, the God we are told loves us becomes a coldhearted king, refusing to heal us, bound to punish us, and ready to announce an eternal prison sentence. In therapeutic salvation, God continues to love us at the time of our death and continues to offer healing love into forever. Dr. Jeff Hopper, one of my theology professors, was once asked, "What happens when we die?" Jeff answered, "I don't know what happens when we die. What I know is that God is love. And because God is love, I trust my life and my death to God." This answer satisfies me. I trust the God who is love in the present will be love in whatever future there may be.

The concept of God as punitive king and its cultural and systemic embodiment does not represent the God I worship. I worship the God who acts with therapeutic salvation, with universal and unconditional lovingkindness. The therapeutic God gives us the gift of creation, the very breath we breathe. The therapeutic God offers forgiveness, reconciliation, and justice. The therapeutic God comes as the Spirit, persuading us to love in healthier ways so we might more fully be alive in peace with all creation. The therapeutic God wants all the cosmos to live in faith, hope, love, and joy. I trust, hope, and rejoice in the salvation offered by the great physician of lovingkindness.

God Is Lovingkindness

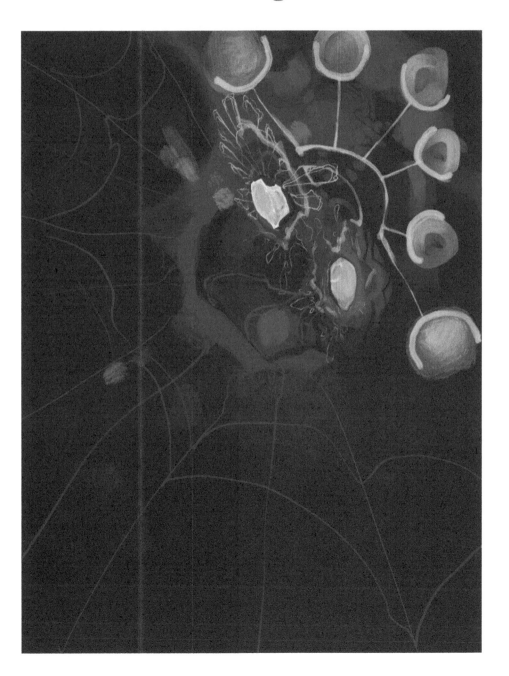

The word "God" is problematic. "God" has been abused and used to abuse. Further, any word or words we use to define what we mean by "God" are inadequate. God is ineffable. If you have a preferred word for the divine energy that creates existence, heals souls, and expands lovingkindness, then I am pleased if you substitute that word where I use "God." I am not bound to the word; I am bound to the energy, the Spirit, that makes life happen in loving ways.

Monotheism generally defines God as Creator and Lord. But why does God create the cosmos and what does the master desire for the cosmos? The word I choose for God is lovingkindness. For me, God is Lovingkindness and Lovingkindness is God. It is not that I think God is in fact lovingkindness or that lovingkindness is God. I repeat, I don't think there are any words that can adequately name God because God is beyond any word. Lovingkindness best expresses how I most fully experience God. My choice is based upon my study of Christian scripture and my experiences in life. Christian scripture is, for me, the family story of encountering God, particularly in the person of Jesus. I interpret and evaluate scripture through my life experiences. I am not a blank page, but a collection of personal and cultural narratives that form my views and direct my behavior. Sometimes scripture challenges my views and sometimes it confirms my views. I find the deepest truth exists where scripture and experience are in alignment.

Now we consider the word "love." In English the word "love" has many forms and uses. "Love" can be a noun (love is kind), a verb (I love you), an adjective (she is a loving person), or an adverb (he gave lovingly). As a verb, "love" has a variety of uses: I love ice cream. I love my friend. I love my family or my group. I love my guest. I love the poor. Greek has a different verb for each of these kinds of love in action and conjugates each of these for person, number, tense, and voice. I simplify the grammar and use the root of each Greek word as a noun, a verb, an adjective, or an adverb without the required Greek inflections or conjugations. My apologies to those who taught me Greek.

Loving ice cream is *eros*. Eros is about what is in it for me. I love ice cream for the pleasure I get out of eating it. The use of the word "eros" can be a problem because in our culture, "erotic," whose root is "eros," commonly refers to something that arouses sexual desire; thus when "eros" is used, sex comes to mind. I use "eros" to indicate the kind of love that appreciates the benefits of an object without forming a relationship with the object. "I love my friend" is *philia*. Philia is a mutually chosen and mutually sustained relationship. When one person decides that the friendship is over, the friendship is over, no matter what the other person feels or wants. Once the mutuality of a relationship is gone, philia is gone. "I love my family or group" is *storge*. Storge is natural or instinctual affection. Storge is most often associated with familial love, but it can also be the bond that ties together a group of people sharing a like-mindedness or an experience, such as members of a political party or fans of a sports team. Storge is what makes us comfortable in one group with whom we identify and uncomfortable with or condemning of another group with whom we don't identify. The power of storge is in shaping our opinions and loyalties, in establishing and confirming our identity, and in forming and confirming our worldviews. "I love my guest" is *xenia*. Xenia is hospitality, and its desire is for the guest to have a good time. A guest is someone invited into our home or sphere of influence. Those who give xenia to their guests provide for their guests' needs, pleasure, and safety.

Finally, there is *agape*. Agape can be a state of being or an action, and I use it as both. As a noun, "agape" is defined as an attitude of concern and generosity. In its verb form, it is defined as acting with or out of charity, and serving love. I translate "agape" as lovingkindness, because agape is about thinking and acting with kindness and concern for another. Agape is unlike eros because it does not ask for anything from the object of its love. Agape is unlike philia because it needs no reciprocal relationship to be sustained. Agape is unlike storge because it reaches outside one's family or identity affiliation. Agape is unlike xenia because it cares for stranger and guest alike. The power of agape is the giving of well-being to those whose well-being is threatened, denied, or stolen.

The Hebrew word for well-being is *shalom* and is most often translated as "peace." It connotes having shelter, food, good health, and joyful relationships. It is a favorite word of Hebrew scripture and is used as a blessing when greeting or parting from someone. The Greek word for well-being is *zoa* and is most often translated as "life." It connotes vitality and abundance. I have chosen the word "well-being" to represent both shalom and zoa. Lovingkindness seeks well-being for all.

In Christian scripture, some form of agape, of being or acting in lovingkindness, is the word translated as "love" when used in relationship to God or to loving one another. When Jesus is asked what is the great commandment of the law, he replies, "You shall act in lovingkindness to the Lord your God with all your heart, and with all your soul, and with all your mind. This is the great and first commandment. And a second is like it, 'You shall act in lovingkindness to your neighbor as yourself.' On these two commandments depend all the law and the prophets."[1] In his Gospel, John writes, "For God so acted in lovingkindness for the cosmos..."[2] Paul wrote to the congregation in Ephesus, "But God, who is rich in mercy, out of the great lovingkindness with which God acted in lovingkindness for us..."[3] And to the church in Rome, Paul writes, "For I am sure that neither death, nor life, nor angels, nor principalities, nor things present, nor things to come, nor powers, nor height, nor depth, nor anything else in all creation, will be able to separate us from the lovingkindness of God in Christ Jesus our Lord."[4] In his first letter, John writes, "You of lovingkindness, let us act in lovingkindness to each other; for lovingkindness is of God, and whoever acts in lovingkindness is born of God and knows God. Whoever does not act in lovingkindness does not know God; for

---

1   Matthew 22:34–40; Mark 12:28–34; Luke 10:25–37. Jesus is quoting Deuteronomy 6:5 and Leviticus 19:18.

2   John 3:16.

3   Ephesians 2:4.

4   Romans 8:38.

God is lovingkindness."[5] To say that God is lovingkindness and acts with lovingkindness is to say that the Divine's desire, purpose, and action is the well-being of creation. To desire another's well-being is to desire that they be well-fed, adequately housed, warmly clothed, in good health, and rich in loving relationships, meaning, purpose, and joy. Whenever I use the word "lovingkindness," I am either translating "agape" from Christian scripture or referring to agape.

God is and acts in lovingkindness not for God's benefit—what God can get out of us—but for our benefit. Lovingkindness is the gift without debt, the sacrifice without recompense, and the forgiveness without deserving. In this understanding, God's desire and purpose is not primarily to be obeyed—though obedience can be a part of the creation's well-being. Nor is it to be adored—though adoration can also be a part of creation's well-being. It at first seemed wrong to me that God's foremost desire is to serve us unconditionally in loving-kindness, without asking anything from us. I had been taught that I was to serve God, not be served by God. That God desires my well-being and is willing to die that I might have peace and abundant life has been and remains somewhat difficult for me to understand or accept. The legalistic and punitive nature of God has attached itself deeply to who I am. But thanks to God's lovingkindness I am, over time, being healed, set free from fear, and hopefully more often *of* lovingkindness.

In my life, my most complex relationships are with my wife and God. My first love for Vickie was a casual philia, a yearlong passing friendship in the college drama department. Philia has proved to be especially important over our last fifty years. Vickie is unquestionably my best friend. One evening, I tried out for a role in *The Diary of Anne Frank*. Vickie was at the audition. I looked across the room, and suddenly I wanted Vickie to love me. The arrow of eros smote me. This, along a circuitous path, eventually led to dating. Philia and eros led us to marriage. Together we came to storge as we built a family and a community, both biologically and relationally, that is the source of

---

5   1 John 4:7–8.

our identity, security, and joy. One of life's great gifts is to offer xenia, hospitality, to our three daughters, their partners, our three grandchildren, and friends.

The glue that holds these various loves together is agape. Vickie has been remarkably faithful in her lovingkindness for me, serving my well-being even when it has been a sacrifice for her. Her career path exemplifies her lovingkindness. She bought and built a preschool and then had to let it go when my bishop moved this itinerant preacher. She adjusted and got her elementary education certification, working her way into being a full-time first-grade teacher. She was a gifted teacher, especially for underprivileged students. But again, she had to let go of her teaching life when the bishop moved me. Yet a third time she built a new career, this time as a Christian educator, only to let it go when I was again moved. More importantly, when I have been at my relational worst, she has continually acted with agape to hold us together. Without her lovingkindness for me, we would not be we.

My initial relationship with God was born of family identity, storge. We were Methodist, and my grandfather was a Methodist pastor. My parents were faithful in their attendance to worship, their private prayers, and their attention to study, works of kindness, and justice. We prayed at meals and before going to bed. We went to Sunday school, vacation bible school, and church summer camps. We practiced generosity for others, giving precious time and 10 percent of my father's small teacher's salary for the well-being of others. We acted together for justice, becoming friends with and supporting the first Black teacher in an all-white Oklahoma high school, visiting a nearby Native American school, and being taught that everyone is a beloved child of God.

My childhood prayers were of an eros-based relationship with God. I had needs I wanted God to fulfill and concerns for others that I wanted God to fix. I had no relationship with God in prayer other than what I wanted from God.

I began to learn how diverse are the understandings of God when in high school I became best friends with two Southern Baptists. On occasion they would invite me to their Sunday school (they earned bonus points for prizes if they brought a guest) or to a revival, and there I learned about a strict and—what seemed to me—harsh version of God as king. I began to recognize that in my own Methodist background there was a less harsh God, but still there was a God who was always judging me based upon either Methodist or Southern Baptist criteria. It was at that time that Bill Satterfield became my pastor. He was a gift of the Spirit. He preached a God of love, of agape. He and I discussed and even argued at youth group meetings. I didn't have full language or understanding, but it was the beginning of a shift that would fill and guide my life.

College came and I decided I wasn't a Christian. I explored other spiritual practices such as Buddhism and Taoism. With new friends, I dabbled in alcohol, and drugs. My philia relationship with God began when, in the summer of 1968, at the age of nineteen and while living in Denver, I read Nikos Kazantzakis's *The Last Temptation of Christ*. The Jesus portrayed by Kazantzakis called to the deepest part of me. I felt Jesus was the kind of person I wanted to be. I wanted to be filled with the Spirit that would drive me to lovingkindness for God and for my neighbor. Feeling this call to my soul, I began to pray the prayer I knew best, the Lord's Prayer, but I found I couldn't remember the next words until I digested the first words. So, I spent time experiencing deeply "Our Father" before I could move to "who art in Heaven." It took an hour or more to fully pray this one simple prayer. This moment was my first experience of the mystical and remains a key moment of mystery and revelation. The image of living and loving like Jesus and the Lord's Prayer became and remain touchstones for my mental and spiritual health.

College, seminary, and postgraduate work in the New Testament was done in the head more than from the heart. It was academically that I was most comfortable approaching an understanding of God.

But while I was being an academic, the Spirit was leading me, unbeknownst to me, by calling me to pastoral ministry as the leader of a series of youth groups. The hospitality of the youths, their parents, and the adult volunteers brought me to a xenia relationship with God through God's people. From them I learned the gifts of being a guest in the home of God.

As a husband, parent, and pastor I came to an agape relationship with God. I came to understand the absolute necessity of lovingkindness for the well-being of my life and all life. Throughout this book I will describe the occasions and nature of lovingkindness that help me to better understand God's lovingkindness for me, and how I might best serve God, my neighbor, and myself.

I confess to an eros love for God. There are things I want from God, like light, breath, and creativity, for my benefit. Only God can give me these things, and I have nothing to offer in return. I confess to a philia love for God, who, over time, has been a trusted friend. I confess to a storge relationship with God in the community of faith that has been critical to the formation of my identity into my eighth decade. The hospitality of xenia is ever present in God and in community. But as in my relationship with Vickie, it is agape—lovingkindness—that is the glue holding together my relationship with God. God gives me lovingkindness day in and day out in creation, in forgiveness and reconciliation, in healing me and using me for the healing of the cosmos. Times of lovingkindness are the best times of my life, my moments of greatest well-being.

THREE

The Gifts of Lovingkindness

We know God's lovingkindness in the gifts God gives us. In Christianity, we have traditionally called these gifts grace. The Greek we render as grace is *charis*. Charis is a gift given for another's benefit. Like agape, it has no strings attached, no ifs, ands, or buts. Grace is a gift freely given for the benefit of the recipient. That God is gracious has deep roots from my childhood, but it was a weekend retreat called Cursillo (Spanish for "short course") that led to further exploration and a subsequent semicoherent articulation. I did not go on the retreat willingly. I had six years of graduate study. I had been a full-time pastor for almost eight years. I didn't want or need a short course in Christianity. Despite my arrogance, I went because a member of the congregation I served kept nagging me. I liked him, but I was getting annoyed by his persistence. So, to shut him up, I agreed to a retreat weekend in September of 1984. It would be a nice getaway, a time to relax. To my surprise, it caused profound and lasting changes in me that were both immediate and the onset of a lifetime of continuing spiritual formation.

The retreat was eclectic in its origins, being an Episcopal Cursillo based upon a Catholic format using United Methodist content. Its eclecticism formed a wonderful coalescing of traditions on being Christian. It was held at Lindisfarne, an Episcopal retreat center on Flathead Lake in Montana. The original Lindisfarne was a monastery on Holy Island off the northeast coast of England. It is a sacred site for

Celtic Christianity. Later you will get the full story of how the Spirit works a mystery between Lindisfarne in Montana and Lindisfarne in England.

The retreat was men only; the women had a separate weekend. For three days we sang, studied, prayed, ate an abundance of good food, relaxed, and worshipped. During study times we were divided into table groups of six. Thirteen talks were given, six by clergy speakers and seven by lay speakers. The talks were wide-ranging, covering an evaluation of how we spend our time and resources, God's various ways of loving us, and tips on spiritual practices to aid us in our discipleship. The clergy talks on the weekend focused on John Wesley's understanding of God's various graces. Following a talk, each table group would discuss the talk's topic and then provide their group's perspective to the others in the room. We closed the weekend with worship and communion that included previous retreatants.

The retreat was, to my surprise, exactly what I needed. I thank the Spirit incarnated in an annoying church member. The long-term effect was to cause me to delve into the life, teaching, and the spiritual practices of John Wesley. John Wesley was not a perfect person, in any sense of perfect. His boils and warts are quickly revealed in his writing and biographies. But John Wesley did not claim to be perfect. He said that God was working in him to heal him so that he might be more perfect in love.

According to Wesley, there are three categories of gifts that align with the Trinity of Creator, Jesus, and the Spirit. Each category gives evidence for a particular gift of lovingkindness, and an opportunity to respond. Below is a chart of Wesley's three categories.

God's Love Evidenced in Grace

Giver	Gift	Love	Response
Creator	Prevenient Grace	Unconditional, Universal	Gratitude
Jesus	Forgiving and Reconciling Grace	Forgiveness, Reconciliation	Acceptance
The Spirit	Perfecting and Sanctifying Grace	Healing, Serving	Cooperation

The first category is God as Creator and is experienced in the creation as prevenient grace, the gift of unconditional and universal love. The second category is God in Jesus and is experienced as forgiving and reconciling grace, the gift of forgiving and reconciling love. The third category is God as the Spirit and is experienced as perfecting and sanctifying grace, the gift of healing and serving love.

Prevenient Grace

Something is prevenient when it precedes us for our benefit. The gift of creation and life is prepared for us before we are born. It is the gift of light and dark, of photosynthesis and quantum mechanics, before we understand or have words for how life happens. It is the gift of new friends waiting around the corner to embrace us for the first time. It is the gift of critters who love us before we know the word love. Jesus says it this way, "Abba makes the sun rise on the evil and on the good, sends rain on the just and on the unjust."[1] All creation, every atom, plant, and person, is a gift from God that precedes us with lovingkindness. Prevenient grace is universal and unconditional lovingkindness.

John Wesley likened prevenient grace to the front porch of God's home. The metaphor is antiquated because not many of us have front porches and if we do, we rarely sit on them. In a time long ago and

---

1   Matthew 5:45.

far, far away, before radio, television, the internet, and cell phones, we would sit on our front porch and view the neighborhood, watching out for the community's safety, calling greetings and grace to one another, taking time to sit and be with each other. Take yourself back to that time and imagine a house with a front porch that thrusts itself into the world. The front porch I imagine has a wide bench swing and a couple of rockers that invite us to sit. It is a gift of shade from the hot sun or the cold rain. It is a place to rest weary bones, and perhaps chat with a new or old friend. It is a place to run toward when we are in danger. The porch is without doors, gates, locks, secret signs, or codes. It sits open to the world, inviting all who would come to find a spell of peace, a place of safety, and a moment of well-being. I experience the joyous gift of God's porch when I walk in the mountains, smell the seasons, hold my child, pet the dog, feel the tenderness of my wife's love, sit by the ocean, stare into the night sky, or sit down to eat.

I know the arguments that creation is the result of causation without intention: that it is a product of probability, that there is no creative energy that persuades life into being, that it is without a desired direction or purpose. Those arguments make no sense to me. I do not understand how everything could come to be without a creative energy—give it whatever name you want—that calls life into being for a desired purpose. But it really doesn't matter what we believe about how the cosmos came to be. Created or not created by some mysterious power, life is given as a universal and unconditional gift.

There is an old story in which God came to visit a brilliant man who was boasting that he didn't need God to create life. God asked the man to show him. So the man took some water and some dirt and began to form it. God said, "Hold on there, get your own water and make your own dirt." The stuff of water and dirt literally comes from the stars. Until we can create our own stars and universe, everything here is gift, is grace, no matter our understanding of how the cosmos came to be. I did not create, nor do I create, what sustains my life. Even my children are not of my making, although I did joyfully cooperate with Vickie in the process.

Wesley recommends that the appropriate response to the gift of creation is gratitude. To be grateful for this gift is to know joy, happiness, and awe in body, mind, heart, and soul. I am grateful for my life. I am grateful for my wife, children, and grandchildren. I am grateful for creation, however that happened. I ground the beginning of each day with a time of prayer that includes a prayer of gratitude, given to me by indigenous spiritual leaders, for creation. For the gift of creation, we are invited to say, "Thank you."

Forgiving and Reconciling Grace

For John Wesley, forgiving grace and reconciling grace are two sides of the same coin. When one is forgiven, one is made right, is reconciled. The Greek word used for forgiveness in the Lord's Prayer, the prayer Jesus taught his disciples to pray, is *aphiemi*. It is the most frequently used Greek word in Christian scripture for forgiveness. "Aphiemi" is defined as to "send forth," "discharge," "send away," "let go," or "set free." Think of a spear thrower. Forgiveness is the action of throwing the spear—the harm—as far away as possible. This aligns with our usual understanding of forgiveness, in which the one who fails love—who sins—is set free from being punished because the failure is "put aside, cast away." For God to forgive our sins is for God to throw our sins away, to send our failures away, to discharge them, to let them go and set us free. God chooses not to define us by or make us pay for our failures to love. Forgiveness is a gift from God.

Forgiveness is not seen by all Christians as gift, as grace. When in the eleventh through thirteenth centuries Western Christianity began to use a form of punitive salvation as its dominant model, forgiveness became conditional. God's forgiveness became reserved for those who jumped through whatever hoop was demanded by those in power. Some folks demand that the "sinner's prayer" be said, others require the confession that "Jesus is my Lord and Savior." For some, to be forgiven one must be baptized in a particular manner at a certain age or behave in a prescribed way or profess a certain creed, dogma, or confession. Some have been taught that before forgiveness can be given there must be repentance (a change of mind or attitude), contrition (an apology), perhaps punishment, and a clear promise to never, ever do it again.

I don't believe that conditional and exclusive forgiveness is the way of Jesus or of lovingkindness. I believe there is nothing I can do to make myself right with God. No apology, no confession, no creed, no ritual act, no sacrifice, nothing of my effort can make me right with God. My only hope is for God to love me, and by that love forgive me, and by that forgiveness return me to a right relationship. When Jesus prayed from the cross, "Abba, forgive them, for they know not what they do,"[2] he was asking Abba that forgiveness be given as a gift, a grace from God, because we don't know what we are doing. Neither Jesus' betrayers nor murderers asked to be forgiven, but Jesus asks Abba to forgive them. Jesus shows us forgiveness as grace, as the way of lovingkindness.

Tragically, forgiveness has been used to abuse people. Too many have been told that forgiving their persecutors means they must stay in death-dealing relationships. In Sunburst, a woman from another congregation came to me. She told me her husband was verbally and physically abusive. She told me his words and described her wounds. I asked if she had gone to her own pastor, and she said she had. She told me her pastor said she must be guilty of causing her husband's anger and that she was clearly not being an obedient wife as the Bible directed. Her pastor told her that not only should she forgive her husband, but she should ask her husband to forgive her for her sins against him. Blaming the victim, making the victim the guilty one, is an old trick of those using their power to sustain abuse. To forgive does not mean remaining the object of abuse, systemic oppression, or structural injustice. Before discussing forgiveness, I ask that the abused one get to a safe place. If there is no safe place from the violence—and for many

---

2   Luke 23:34.

there is no safe place—then find a safe person or people. Once safe the abused may forgive, pray, and work for the well-being of an abuser, but only when safe. I want to be very clear that if someone is in an abusive relationship or situation, they should get to safety ASAP before working on what forgiveness might be in their situation.

In therapeutic salvation, Jesus' death is an act of forgiveness, of sacrificial lovingkindness. Jesus could have fled Jerusalem and escaped his unjust and cruel death. Jesus does not want to die. But Jesus stays because Jesus loves his friends and his enemies. Jesus chooses to let his life be taken that friend and enemy might see the death caused by failed lovingkindness. Abba answers Jesus' prayer from the cross by forgiving those disciples who betray Jesus at his arrest, by forgiving those who unjustly brought Jesus to trial, by forgiving those who ridicule and abuse Jesus on his way to crucifixion, and by forgiving those who kill Jesus. Even when we murder God's love made flesh, God declares unconditional, universal, and forgiving love as gift. God's forgiveness throws our cruelty into sharp view and then throws it far from us. Though our failure to love is despicable, God restores us to lovingkindness. The most basic understanding by Christians of Jesus' resurrection is as a sign of God's forgiveness and victory over our failures to love. By forgiving us, God declares our relationship with God to be right, to be reconciled, and we are restored to lovingkindness by God's lovingkindness.

I barely understand a love so great that it submits to being murdered by human failure and then forgives the murderer. The closest I come to this kind of love is in being a parent. When my children were young, I would gladly have taken their suffering upon me. When they fell, I wished the bloody scrape could be mine. Many parents have said to me that they too would rather suffer than see their children suffer. And parents who have blessed me by including me in their lives as their child suffers and dies have all said they would rather the suffering and death be theirs. This includes a mother and father of a three-year-old child who died of a brain tumor. It includes a mother who, at

101, mourned it should have been her when her eighty-two-year-old daughter died. Parents would rather die than have their children suffer. So it is, apparently, with God.

My daughter's teething was difficult. When she was one and a half years old, I once sat in a bathtub with her while she repeatedly threw up on me. I would have gratefully taken on her pain that she might be spared the suffering. When one of my daughters at two years old decided to be a big girl and take her own medicine, I called the Poison Control Center, and as they instructed, I gave her an emetic. I then held her while she projectile vomited. I wished it were me vomiting. When our young children entered the trials of being three and said, "I hate you," though wounded to tears, Vickie and I threw their words as far away as possible and continued to feed them, house them, and love them. When in adolescence our daughters picked fights with their mother in their growth toward independence, though deeply hurt, we did not hold it against them but loved them. And on it goes with each child. If I am to remain their loving Pop, then my willingness to be wounded and to forgive is essential. None of this makes me exceptional. I did what most every parent does in lovingkindness for their children.

I want to be clear that I have wounded and been forgiven more often than I have forgiven. Early in their childhood, when I wanted my children to do or say what I wanted them to do or say and the moment devolved into a confrontational power struggle, I used my anger, my big, loud, harsh voice, and my greater strength to force them into submission. Yet I was forgiven. When we were backpacking in the high mountains, I pushed them hard to carry their packs and keep going because they needed to be tough to meet the challenges of life. Only later did I learn that they had exercise-induced asthma and they literally couldn't carry their backpacks and breathe at ten thousand feet. I was harshly driving them against their own body wisdom. Yet I was forgiven. My sins in failing to act in lovingkindness for my children are legion. The only reason we are still in a loving relationship is because they have chosen to forgive me. The same forgiveness has been necessary in my marriage and in my ministry.

In these small ways, I understand the love of God that gives the forgiveness that is essential to be in right relationship with God. God forgives us and continues to love us despite our failures to love and our ways of death, both large and small, literal and metaphorical. In lovingkindness God chooses to say, "I agape you and I forgive you. You are right with me, and I love you onward."

Perfecting and Sanctifying Grace

At the ordination of a United Methodist pastor, a bishop asks of those being ordained the nineteen questions that John Wesley asked Methodist preachers. Some of the questions are difficult to answer, such as question eighteen: "Are you in debt so as to embarrass you in your work?" The desired answer is "No." Many pastors come out of the educational process with significant debt, but being embarrassed by debt is a personal response. I was not embarrassed.

Questions two, three, and four are about perfection.

2. Are you going on to perfection?
3. Do you expect to be made perfect in love in this life?
4. Are you earnestly striving after it?

One of the struggles of my life has been the need to appear perfect. Such perfectionism is one of the reasons I numbed my fear of failure by excessively drinking alcohol. It is also why I lied about insignificant things just to look good. But this understanding of wanting to be perfect has nothing to do with John Wesley's question about "going on to perfection."

What Wesley was asking of Methodist preachers was, "Is God as the Spirit, active in making you kinder and more loving? Is God perfecting love in you? Do you trust God and strive for God's perfecting of you in love?" Wesley experienced that cooperating with the Spirit changed his life and the lives of others toward being more often of lovingkindness. He attributed this change to the perfecting grace of God. He wanted his preachers to also know and claim the perfecting grace of God.

Perfecting grace is a healing grace in which the gap between the lovingkindness we are created to be and our failures in being lovingkindness is narrowed. By God's perfecting grace we are more often persons of lovingkindness. I believe, that by the grace of God, I am (one) going on to perfection and, (two) expect to become more loving in this life as (three) I earnestly strive to cooperate with the Spirit.

Related to perfecting grace is sanctifying grace. "To sanctify" means "to dedicate to the use of God." Sanctifying grace is the gift by which we are dedicated and purposed to be used as an instrument of God for lovingkindness. In the schema of therapeutic salvation, to be perfected and sanctified by the Spirit is to be shaped into a more loving person who is used for acts of lovingkindness. By the gifts of perfecting and sanctifying grace, we become partners with God for the well-being of the cosmos.

We will spend more time with prevenient, forgiving and reconciling, and perfecting and sanctifying grace later. For now, it is important to understand that God as lovingkindness is revealed in the gifts God gives. Prevenient grace is the God-given gift of unconditional and universal lovingkindness in creation. Forgiving and reconciling grace are the God-given gifts of forgiveness and reconciled relationships as revealed and modeled in Jesus. Perfecting and sanctifying grace are God-given gifts through the Spirit. They are the healing love we need to grow and act in lovingkindness for God, each other, ourselves, and creation. It has been thirty-eight years since the unwanted Cursillo retreat set me on a journey into the gifts of lovingkindness. I am still learning to unwrap and live God's gifts.

─ F O U R ─

We Are Lovingkindness

Those who have a different understanding than mine of God will have a different understanding of what it means to be human. I speak of my understanding. For me, Jesus embodies what it looks like for God's lovingkindness to be made flesh. Jesus is not the exclusive embodiment of lovingkindness for me but is my best teacher and the model of living lovingkindness I wish to emulate.

Genesis 1:27 says, "God created humankind in God's image, in the image of God, God created them." If, as I believe, God is lovingkindness and revealed in acts of lovingkindness, then to say we are made in the image of God is to say we are made to be and act in lovingkindness. Made in the image of lovingkindness, we are our most authentic selves when we give ourselves to each other and the world with unconditional, universal, forgiving, reconciling, perfecting, and sanctifying grace. Like God, our primary purpose in life is the well-being of our fellow beings, of ourselves, of the creation. By our actions of lovingkindness, we unite with God in creating well-being.

My life has been filled with those who have been lovingkindness to me. A strong image of lovingkindness is my grandmother Orendorff, who we called Mom. Mom, widowed in her sixties, lived alone in a one-bedroom, one-bath house in Cherryvale, Kansas. When my parents and their five kids came to visit, we filled the house with noise, high energy, and needs for food and places to sleep. Yet when we came, she always stood on her front porch, smiling almost to laughter, ready, yearning to give us lovingkindness. And when we left, she was again on

her front porch; this time tears coursed down her cheeks. Not yet out of her dirt driveway, she already missed us.

People of lovingkindness seem to appear when I need them. The summer between my sixth and seventh grades, our family moved from Ponca City, Oklahoma, to Warrensburg, Missouri. The next summer we moved from Warrensburg to Casper, Wyoming. For me, the moves compounded the confusion typical of adolescence. Somehow, perhaps because of my Southern accent, at East Junior High School in Casper I was identified by a tough group of boys as Goon. Goon became their name for me. Sometimes at lunch they would chase me, knock me down, rough me up, pull my underwear up from behind, and laugh, singing, "Nooky, nooky, Goon." It got so that on school mornings I became nauseous. Worse, I began to believe I was Goon.

In ninth grade I read William Glasser's *Reality Therapy,* a book my father left lying on a table. Glasser said we are beings who need to love, to be loved, and to have purpose. This truth struck me and changed me. My purpose became loving and being loved, even if I was Goon. That summer I worked as a custodian at Casper College and one of the college students, Paul Halley, and I became friends. Paul saw and treated me as a person of interest and worth. He liked me and liked being with me. I was not Goon to him, and because of his acceptance I was not Goon to the rest of the crew. I began to see myself as a person of worth, as a friend, as lovable, even if there was a part of me that was Goony. William Glasser and Paul Halley are two of a long line of those who have come to me as lovingkindness incarnate.

In the traditional model of punitive salvation, we are born Goon, irredeemably bad and deserving of eternal punishment. The official name of this church doctrine is original sin. Matthew Fox, a defrocked Catholic priest, disputes the doctrine of original sin in his book *Original Blessing.* He quotes Genesis 1:31, which says, "God saw everything God had made, and indeed, it was very good." Fox holds that we are not born Goon; we are born good, even very good. According to Genesis 1:31, our origin is not a curse, but a blessing. Our created nature is not rot and wormwood, but a divinely blessed goodness. Brené Brown, a research sociologist, makes a similar observation in her work on shame and guilt. Shame is when, after I mess up, I say, "I am a bad person. I am Goon." Which is to say, there is something fundamentally bad about me. Guilt is to say, "I messed up." Which is to say, I am fundamentally a good person who has messed up.

In therapeutic salvation, we are made in the image of God as lovingkindness. We are not bad people who occasionally do good. We are loving people who occasionally fail to act with lovingkindness. When we fail to be lovingkindness, then we need forgiveness and help from the Spirit to again be our truest selves.

Just as God loves us for our benefit, so also, as our best selves, do we love God for God's benefit. To offer lovingkindness to God is to become servants of God's lovingkindness. To act in lovingkindness to God is to offer whatever heart, mind, soul, and strength we have to God for the ongoing well-being of creation. In acting with lovingkindness, we choose to be partners with God—very junior partners to be sure, but nonetheless partners in creating well-being for creation.

Jesus tells us that loving God is the same as loving our neighbor as we love ourselves. We offer lovingkindness to our neighbor not for our benefit, but for our neighbor's well-being. We love our neighbor and our enemy not because it feels good, or because there is some reward in it, or even from enlightened self-interest, but because our neighbor needs our care and our forgiveness, because our enemy needs our compassion and our service for their well-being. Loving our neighbor as ourselves means we are made to act for our neighbor's well-being.

Loving others as God loves us also means we forgive others as God forgives us. I am not always forgiving. I can be defensive, angry, accusatory, and resentful. Wounded, I am unable to make myself forgive the one who wounds. I hang on to, even nurture, my anger and resentment. I need the Spirit's help. For me the most effective way to forgive others has been prayer. As I struggled in a particularly difficult time, a time when I was betrayed by a colleague, a betrayal that cost me friendships, my job, and mental health, the Spirit gave me an insight. The Spirit suggested that when I was in a time of nursed resentment and anger, I should pray for the well-being of the one who betrayed me. At first this simple shift was difficult. I didn't want the betrayer's well-being; I wanted them to get their comeuppance. I wanted them to be punished and to suffer, if not eternally, then at least for a very miserable and very long time. But because the Spirit said to, and because praying well-being for the one I needed to forgive seemed the right thing to do, and because I was tired of the pain I was causing myself and others, without sincerity I obediently prayed for their well-being. I shifted my focus from my wound and toward their healing. It was a mental shift and substitution that surprisingly worked. Over time, and not that much time, my anger and resentment were gone. I was freed of their power to harm me. By praying for the well-being of my perceived enemy, I was freed of the death spiral of rehashed resentment. Forgiving them came as a byproduct of praying lovingkindness for them.

I confess that I still don't want those who repeatedly harm me and others to be an active part of my life. I repeat myself in saying that victims of abuse can forgive the abuser, but they must never, ever think that forgiveness means permitting the abuse, whether physical, mental, or spiritual, to continue. There are persons in my life from whose presence I abstain because they are dangerous to me. However, I can, from a safe distance, work in lovingkindness for their well-being.

Made in the image of God, we also need to love and forgive ourselves. We offer lovingkindness to ourselves not because we are always lovable but because we need to care for ourselves, forgive ourselves, and be open to the healings offered to us. We forgive ourselves, just as God forgives us, not because we deserve forgiveness, but because we need forgiveness as a gift.

Being created in the image of God carries responsibility for the well-being of the whole of creation. Right after God says, "Let us make humankind in our image," God says, "They shall care for the fish of the sea, the birds of the sky, the cattle, the whole earth."[1] I believe that creation is one fantastic organism and that lovingkindness holds me responsible for the well-being of that organism, or at least my acre of the cosmos. The creatures of my life, particularly the dogs and cats that have lived with me, who have needed my care and kindness, have taught me much about loving and being loved. The flowers and the fruit of my garden, the wind and the birds who fly upon it, the sea as I sail across it, the high mountain trail and the planets and stars as I gaze heavenward, ask for my lovingkindness, and teach me that to be alive is to be lovingkindness for the well-being of all creation.

To be human is to know that I am made in the image of God and that my being is, as God says, "very good." In Wesleyan terms, I am made to be universal, unconditional, forgiving, reconciling, perfecting, and sanctifying lovingkindness. If a greater explanation of being human is needed, read chapter 2 again, only this time, imagine the description of God's various ways of loving as a description of how we are made to love. We are made in the image of God, in the image of lovingkindness, and that is very good.

---

1   Genesis 1:28.

FIVE

The Dreaded Word (Sin)

For years I hated the word "sin." It carried connotations of innate human depravity and judgmental condemnation. Yet it was squarely in the middle of the theology and culture in which I grew up. By this understanding I was, from the core, wicked and dirty. As a child, when I didn't share or I got angry, I was sin. My hormonal thirst for sex as an adolescent revealed that I was sin. My adult wandering eye and lust for power and recognition confirmed I was sin.

Human depravity is one possible meaning of "sin," but there are other meanings. Learning to read biblical Greek changed my understanding of sin. The Greek word we translate into English as "sin" is *hamartia*. The definition of the noun form of "hamartia" is "a failure, error, sin." And the definition of the verb form of "hamartia" is "to miss, miss the mark...to fail of doing, fail of one's purpose, go wrong." The word "sin" often carries, for us, a connotation of evil. But hamartia is not necessarily evil; it is simply failing to achieve an intended goal or purpose.

If to sin is to miss the mark or fail of one's purpose, then what constitutes sin is dependent on what we aim to accomplish. If the target is to be rich, then it is a sin to be poor. If the target is to be funny and no one laughs, that is a sin. I like the analogy of an archer, who, when they miss their target, has sinned. The question for us, as we try to understand what sin means, is "What is the target at which we aim? What is the purpose which we intend?" If the target is a certain set of laws and we fail to keep those laws, then we miss the mark and that is sin. If the target is to agree with a certain creedal statement or dogma and we fail to agree, we miss the mark and that is sin. My reading of Paul, the Gospels, and early church history leads me to believe that wealth, humor, rules, creeds, and dogma are not the target at which Jesus, or the early Christians, aimed. In fact, there were no creedal statements until the fourth century CE, and those were written by some church leaders for the convenience and at the insistence of Emperor Constantine. Jesus clearly sets the target for his followers when he is asked, "What is the first or most important commandment?" and he answers, as previously noted, that the first commandment is "to agape the Lord your God with all your heart, with all your mind, with all your soul and with all your strength." And Jesus says the second is the same as the first, "to agape your neighbor as yourself." To be lovingkindness and to act in lovingkindness to God, neighbor, and self is the target named by Jesus. For Jesus, to sin is to miss the target of lovingkindness.

Paul names the same target to the congregation in Galatia: "For the whole law is fulfilled in one word, 'You shall agape your neighbor as yourself.'"[1] John writes in his first letter to the churches: "Beloved, since God loved us so much, we also ought to love one another. No one has ever seen God; if we love one another, God lives in us, and God's love is perfected in us."[2] Each time John mentions love, he is speaking of lovingkindness. The target is lovingkindness. Sin is missing or failing to be lovingkindness. When we fail to be and act in lovingkindness, when we fail to agape God, our neighbor, and ourselves for well-being, then we miss the target. It is no accident that the first followers of Jesus called themselves "people of the way"[3] rather than Christian. They heard Jesus' call to live lovingkindness as the way to follow him. They believed that by their efforts to imitate Jesus and with the aid of the Spirit, they would be perfected in the way of lovingkindness.

When I fail to live and love like Jesus, I have missed the target, I have failed to live in the way of Jesus, and I have sinned. The consequence of my failure to act in lovingkindness is broken relationships and a broken world. With sin I create a barrier, a separation from family, friends, community, the Earth, and God. Broken relationships are a deep source of pain and suffering. I am miserable when I sin. But the consequences of sin are not primarily about me. When I fail to "love as God first loved me,"[4] I create misery for creation and all its members. When I sin, I fail to be a source of healing and I become a source of suffering. My failure is destructive to universal well-being.

---

1   Galatians 5:14.
2   1 John 4:7–8, 11–12.
3   Acts 9:2.
4   1 John 4:19.

I don't want to wound or destroy, so I try to be more like the lovingkindness I see in Jesus. Sometimes my attempts succeed. Sometimes, even when I am willing to love, I fail. Paul writes in his letter to the church in Rome, "I do not understand my own actions. For I do not do what I want, but I do the very thing I hate."[5] Some parts of me are so broken that I, like Paul, sin when I don't want to sin. I say words I wish I hadn't said, words that harm and are hard to heal. Even as a drunk, I knew I should stop drinking, but I didn't until I was sick and tired of being sick and tired. More confounding is that sometimes when I am convinced that I am loving, I am in truth failing, I am sinning. When I was driving my daughters to carry their backpacks high in the mountains, I thought I was loving them, but I was harming them.

Sin divides and isolates us from those and that which love unites. Without lovingkindness marriages fail, friendships fail, parents fail. Without lovingkindness we suffer in body, mind, and spirit, as we harshly judge ourselves, despise ourselves, condemn ourselves, and destroy ourselves. Without lovingkindness the social and institutional fabric, which makes life successful and safe, fails. Without lovingkindness creation fails. Without lovingkindness there is no well-being.

Paul writes to Rome's struggling congregation, "For the consequence of our failure to act in lovingkindness is death, but the free gift of God is a life of well-being in all times; a gift given to us in Jesus."[6] Paul knows the consequence of sin is death. He also wants the believers in Rome to know that they are not trapped in the death of their failures, but that God forgives them and offers them lovingkindness in every moment, and that they can do the same for each other.

My point in this chapter is that sin is the target we miss, the purpose we fail, not the rotten state of our souls or the failure to keep human-interpreted divine rules, dogma, or creed. The target and

---

5   Romans 7:15.

6   Romans 6:23.

purpose, as set by Jesus, is to live lovingkindness toward God, others, and ourselves. Sin, that dreaded word, is our failure to be lovingkindness.

In subsequent chapters I will address the process by which we are healed and restored by the Creator, Jesus, and the Spirit into persons who are more often of lovingkindness, persons who may be used by the Spirit for healing our communities and the creation. For now, know that God gifts us with lovingkindness even when we fail to be lovingkindness.

We Have a Choice

When I was in sixth grade, my parents gave me money as a Christmas gift. I didn't want money. I didn't know what I wanted, but it wasn't money. Money was a lousy gift. I said so angrily and stomped out of the room. I rejected their gift of love. As painful as my ingratitude must have been, my parents didn't take the money back. They left it under the Christmas tree, in the envelope with my name on it, until I decided what I would do. When receiving a gift, we have choices. We can express gratitude, say nothing, or berate the gift, as I did. We can accept the gift or refuse it. We can use the gift in our lives or store it at the back of the closet or even throw it away.

The God of my understanding constantly offers gifts to us. God's gifts are greater than money at Christmas. God's gifts are the therapy we need to grow in lovingkindness for well-being. God's gifts can help us to fail less often and succeed to be and act in lovingkindness more often. God as Creator offers us the gift of life. We choose to be grateful, indifferent, or ungrateful. God in Jesus offers forgiving and reconciling love. We choose to accept, ignore, or refuse God's forgiveness. In every moment God as the Spirit offers us new wisdom and new ways for well-being. We choose to cooperate or not to cooperate with the Spirit. Wesley's understanding of grace has been called responsible grace because we are given the choice of how we respond to each of God's gifts. A positive response more fully opens us to the healing of the Spirit.

God's love is such that if we choose ingratitude, refusal, or non-cooperation, God continues to love us and continues to come to us in lovingkindness. God does not give up on us, even when we may have given up on ourselves, or given up on God. A favorite phrase for Carl Jung was "Invoked or uninvoked, God is present." Richard Rohr, a Catholic priest and author, has often said, "We're already in the presence of God. What's absent is our awareness." I say, "The sunset is present whether or not we take time to notice, feel awe, and enjoy its beauty." God's love for us is not dependent on our acknowledgment or our response. God's love is universal and unconditional. But our awareness and experience of God's love is dependent on our choices, our responses.

Our power to choose to respond to God's love is one of Wesley's most controversial ideas. During the time and place of John Wesley, the predominant thought was that humanity was so corrupt that it was impossible for any human to make a sinless decision. Every choice any human made was flawed, sin-filled. This led to the idea that only God can make the choice for us and so God selected, or elected, some for Heaven and did not select others, who then were sent to Hell. For me, the concept of this special selection or election, to choose some for Heaven and to condemn others to eternal damnation, is incompatible with a God whose love is universal and unconditional, forgiving, and reconciling.

In Greek, the words translated as "election" are *eklektos* and *ekloge*. Both mean "laid out, chosen or choice." Theologians have, in general, offered two understandings. The elect are either those God has chosen for Heaven or Hell, or those God has chosen for a particular task at a particular time. I believe it is a misreading of the text to understand the elect as God's specially chosen people for a special place in an afterlife. I suggest that "elect" be read with a mindset of therapeutic salvation rather than of punitive salvation, so that one is gifted and selected to do one thing, and another is gifted and selected to do something else for the well-being of the world. Such diversity of election creates the community of many gifts we need for well-being. This is the thrust of Paul's writing in 1 Corinthians 12 on the varieties of gifts, service, and working, each of which is needed for the well-being of the whole body. Paul writes, "Now there are varieties of gifts, but the one Spirit; and there are varieties of service, but the one Lord; and there are varieties of working, but it is the same God who inspires them all in everyone."[1]

In my family there is a diversity of gifts and elections. I believe I was made and elected to be a pastor. My twin sister is a great CPA and dancer. She has done lovingkindness with her election in both areas.

---

1   1 Corinthians 12:4–6.

One brother, who sadly died at a young age, was a remarkable engineer and project manager. Another brother is a gifted athlete and mentor. My younger sister has been elected to practice lovingkindness as a consultant with an international corporation. The concept that each of us is gifted and, by our gifts, called to a healing work for all of us is consistent with a therapeutic understanding of election.

However, we are, as Carl Jung in his writing on being a psychoanalyst and Henri Nouwen in his writing on spirituality remind us, "wounded healers." It is self-evident that we are broken and flawed and so any decision we make is broken and flawed. Still, no matter how flawed our choice may be, a choice to turn toward and open ourselves to God's love opens us to God's healing, which then opens us to being used in God's healing of the world. E. Stanley Jones, a Methodist missionary, writes in his book *The Divine Yes* that our yes to God is small but God's Divine Yes is big, perfecting and sanctifying of our smallness. Process theology says that God's love is persuasive and not coercive. God's love persuades us, imperfect as we are, to enter a process of being made kinder and more loving.

As I have said, Wesley spoke of God's prevenient grace, God's love gifted through the creation, as a porch inviting us to come and sit, to be safe and at peace. We can choose to sit on God's porch and be grateful for our lives and world or we can play in the traffic. If we choose God's porch, we may sit crooked, deaf, and poor sighted, but we are on God's porch. We recognize the porch as a gift, and with gratitude we choose to rest our flawed and weary selves.

Wesley spoke of God's forgiveness and reconciliation as a door into the home of God. We can choose to walk through the door by accepting God's forgiveness for us. Our entrance into God's home may be with a limp, it may be backward, it may be in a wheelchair or on a stretcher carried by friends; we may be drugged out, or we may simply trip and fall; but however flawed our entrance, we are forgiven, we go through God's door of forgiveness, and we enter the home of God.

Wesley spoke of perfecting and sanctifying grace as a life lived in the home of God. We can choose to live inside God's home with gratitude for the universal and unconditional love of the Creator evidenced in the creation. We can choose to accept God's forgiveness and be reconciled. We can choose to use our lives to seek justice for the least and the oppressed. We can choose to share breath with the Spirit, who heals our broken souls and uses us to heal others, who teaches us wisdom and makes use of us for the joy of others. We can choose to live in the home of God, where bread is shared with all who are hungry. Our life inside the home of God will be flawed. We will burn the toast, glare in anger and anguish, and speak harshly. We will have moments of selfishness and cruelty. But no matter how flawed we are, we have chosen to live inside God's home, where we make ourselves present to the graces of God in creation, Jesus, and the Spirit for the well-being of the world.

In my life it has not been the correctness or purity of my choices that has mattered. When in 1968 I decided I wanted to follow Jesus, that I wanted to live and love like Jesus, I was a selfish adolescent on drugs. When in 1977 I decided I was called to be a pastor, a portion of my motivation was the desires to finish my dissertation, to change people to whom I thought they should be, and to earn money for my wife and baby girl. What has been important is that however imperfect I am and however imperfect my decision, I remain open to God's love healing me that I might be more fully used for lovingkindness. I don't need to be perfect. I don't need to get the choice right. I need to stay in love with God and let God use my imperfections and my choices to grow lovingkindness.

God uses our choices, imperfect as they may be, to heal us, and by healing us, heal creation. After ten years of serving a large congregation, I needed a rest. I was burned-out, grumpy, and becoming ineffective. I considered taking a year off or quitting pastoral ministry altogether. A staff member suggested I do a pulpit exchange to another country through the World Methodist Federation. It sounded like something I would enjoy and was something my family could do with me. Furthermore, it was something that would give me a break from the current pressures. I chose to apply to the World Methodist Federation's exchange program. I didn't tell the WMF that I was burned-out and grumpy and probably should not be anyone's pastor. In their application, the WMF asked questions to help them find an appropriate exchange. I told them what I wanted. I wanted an English-speaking congregation because English is my only fluent language. I wanted Great Britain or Australia so my daughters of high school age would be most comfortable. I wanted something near London for the museums and theater. These were my imperfect and selfish choices. The Spirit used my flawed self and choices in surprising ways.

The exchange to which I was assigned was in Hexham, Northumberland, England. Hexham is near Hadrian's Wall and almost in Scotland. It is as rural as England gets. It is near no theater, no library, and no significant museum, and there was not much for my family to do. I asked for a small congregation. I was assigned three small congregations, of which I was the primary pastor, and I was placed on the circuit, meaning I had to travel multiple times a week to other towns and a variety of congregations. I was a curiosity as the pastor from Montana. Thankfully, the people did speak English, but it was not Montana English. On the first Sunday, after worship, a couple came to us and asked, and I quote, "Would you like to come to our home for a joint and a bit of crack?" This was not the English or Methodism to which I was accustomed. It turned out that "joint" is a cut of meat and "crack" is conversation. My request for a pulpit exchange looked like a failure for the whole family.

I needed healing, and I thought I knew how that healing should happen. The Spirit knew better than I what healing I needed, transforming my flawed wants into gifts. Once in Northumberland, we developed new friendships that we still cherish. I discovered I could be both deeply spiritual and a social activist. We were inspired by people of faith and their stories. At one of the study groups, I was introduced to Celtic Christianity. Celtic Christianity precedes Roman Christianity in Ireland, Scotland, and northern England. The Celtic aspect comes from the indigenous spirituality of the Irish and the Scots. It is an animism built upon a universal Spirit. The Christian aspect most likely comes from Christian men and women who lived in the deserts of Egypt, often called the desert mothers and fathers. Celtic Christian spirituality combined for me what I loved about the spirituality of the Salish and Kootenai peoples back in Polson, Montana, with whom we spent four years, and what I loved about the way of Jesus. I reveled in the stories of the Celtic saints and their art, poetry, prayer, and music. We visited sacred sites, including Iona and Lindisfarne. Do you remember Lindisfarne on Flathead Lake and the Cursillo I attended ten years earlier? For a second time I was healed and renewed at Lindisfarne, this time by the Celtic Christians. I returned to Montana a rich, rich man with new energy for ministry.

By the way, I ended up keeping the money my parents gave me for Christmas. I apologized to them, and they gently forgave me. They listened and helped me understand the confusion of being an adolescent whose raging hormones made for emotional overreaction. They helped me understand that it was natural for me to not yet be sure of what I wanted or where I was going. My reaction to their gift must have wounded them, but they didn't tell me that. They remained loving, forgiving, and gracious. Years later I reminded my mother of that sixth-grade Christmas. She didn't remember anything about it. She loved me then and she loved me years later.

Even though we are imperfect and our choices are flawed, the Spirit uses us and our decisions to heal us in lovingkindness that we might know well-being and be instruments of lovingkindness for the world. I am not now fully perfected in love nor fully sanctified as an instrument of lovingkindness, but I believe I am better and getting better at being lovingkindness, not because I am a good person or because I make good choices, but because I strive to be grateful for life, to accept forgiveness, and to cooperate with the Spirit. To choose to live in the home of God, to choose to cooperate with the Spirit in the process being healed and restored to our best selves is to choose therapeutic salvation.

SEVEN

Responding to the Gifts

We have been given great gifts of life, of forgiveness and reconciliation, and of the Spirit. As said, we can choose how we respond to God's gifts. John Wesley directs the first Methodists toward three fundamental responses: gratitude for life, acceptance of forgiveness, and cooperation with the Spirit. In this chapter, we examine gratitude and acceptance. In following chapters, we will consider cooperation with the Spirit.

Gratitude

At our home we say a prayer at the evening meal. It is a sacred ritual I learned as a child. When I pray almost anything can come out of my mouth, but it always includes thank you and a request for our healing and the healing of the world. Vickie's prayer is always the same; it is something she learned as a child and is an anchor to her life. She prays, "Bless us, O Lord, for these gifts which we are about to receive, and may they produce in us peace, love, harmony, and understanding." Both of us acknowledge that the lives we have are gifts, from the food on the table to our shared presence, for the well-being of the world. Being grateful to the power that makes and sustains life is the act of saying thank you for life. Life is a precious, fragile, and amazing gift. It is free. It is simply given to us. "Thank you" seems too easy, but it is the best response we can give.

Viewing life with gratitude is meant to become a habit of seeing the many gifts of our existence. Every year I plant tomatoes, they grow themselves, and I harvest with gratitude. I am grateful that I have been present at the miracle of one of my children's and one of my grandchildren's births, and I say thank you. I say thank you for my telescope when I see craters on the moon, the rings of Saturn, or the Orion nebula. Daily Vickie blesses me, my children and grandchildren bless me, my friends and neighbors bless me. Strangers who built my house and grew the food on my table bless me. Even my enemies bless me with gifts of life. Every night when I have settled down to sleep, I begin my prayers by naming the day's blessings and saying thank you for each.

Being grateful changes our stance to life by shifting our focus away from grasping for our desire. The opposite of being grateful is whining. Whining is focusing on what we don't have, didn't get, or had stolen. Whining spirals downward into a black pit of self-pity, anger, resentment, and depression. In gratitude, we focus on our blessings. Gratitude heals our hearts, our souls, and the world. There have been several interesting psychological, sociological, biochemical, and neurological studies on gratitude. The bottom line is that practicing gratitude results in better physical and mental health, an increased likelihood to exercise, increased self-control, stronger feelings of belonging, fewer feelings of loneliness, better relationships, and a reduction in stress. Gratitude leads to hope and healthy hormones caressing our brain and body. We count our blessings not just because our grandmothers told us to but because counting blessings, being grateful, makes our sleep more restful and our waking more joyful.

Acceptance

The appropriate response to forgiving and reconciling grace is acceptance. Forgiveness and reconciliation, like all divine gifts, are freely given. They are not something we earn or can command from God. God's choice to act with forgiveness makes us right, reconciles us, with God and leads to our reconciliation with others. The question is not "Are we forgiven?" but "Do we choose to accept that we are forgiven?"

Will we accept that the Creator of the cosmos throws our sin away? Will we, having failed to love, accept that "Jesus loves me, this I know"? We are not required to accept forgiveness. Nor are we required to accept being reconciled with God. We can choose to ignore the gifts as if they didn't exist. We can acknowledge the gifts of existence but refuse to open them. Or we can choose to accept the gifts of forgiveness and reconciliation, open them, and live in them.

To accept forgiveness and reconciliation, we need to admit that we need forgiveness, that we need to be reconciled, that we have failed to be and act in lovingkindness. Admitting we need forgiveness is an act of confessing that we have caused harm. Such an admission can be difficult because our human brain is quick at writing history to our advantage and amazing at self-justification, saying, with convicted certitude, "I am innocent and the victim of another's sin." Accepting forgiveness also requires repentance, the need to change our mind from self-justification to admitting that we have done harm. This change of thinking, with its necessary behavior changes, is often more than we can do on our own. We need the help of the Spirit to have our minds changed so we are more often of lovingkindness. Accepting forgiveness requires seeking reconciliation with those we have wounded when that is possible. The purpose of forgiveness is to heal broken relationships. The twelve steps of Alcoholics Anonymous[1] offer a concise process for accepting forgiveness and the power of reconciliation to awaken us spiritually. Though step one is about alcohol, it could be about any of our failures to be lovingkindness.

1. We admitted we were powerless over alcohol—that our lives had become unmanageable.
2. Came to believe that a Power greater than ourselves could restore us to sanity.
3. Made a decision to turn our will and our lives over to the care of God as we understood God.
4. Made a searching and fearless moral inventory of ourselves.

---

1 *Alcoholics Anonymous*, 4th ed. (New York: Alcoholics Anonymous World Services, Inc., 2001).

5. Admitted to God, to ourselves, and to another human being the exact nature of our wrongs.

6. Were entirely ready to have God remove all these defects of character.

7. Humbly asked God to remove our shortcomings.

8. Made a list of all persons we had harmed and became willing to make amends to them all.

9. Made direct amends to such people wherever possible, except when to do so would injure them or others.

10. Continued to take personal inventory and when we were wrong promptly admitted it.

11. Sought through prayer and meditation to improve our conscious contact with God, as we understood God, praying only for knowledge of God's will for us and the power to carry that out.

12. Having had a spiritual awakening as the result of these Steps, we tried to carry this message to alcoholics, and to practice these principles in all our affairs.

To accept the forgiveness of God and others is to empty ourselves before God's mercy that we might be merciful toward ourselves, others, and all creation. What we cannot do for ourselves, the Spirit does in us. To accept being forgiven by God is to accept the gift of being reconciled with God. By accepting God's gift of forgiveness, we more often forgive family, friend, enemy, and ourselves. God gives us the power to make this choice. God offers us agency to accept forgiveness and to forgive as we are forgiven. To trust that the power that made us continues to love us and create love in us even when we fail to love is to accept forgiveness and be reconciled.

Being grateful is saying thank you that the creation in which we live is built upon universal and unconditional lovingkindness. Accepting forgiveness is claiming our freedom from the shame of our failures so we are free to love anew. I am grateful for the lovingkindness that gives me life, and I strive to love as I have been loved. I accept the

lovingkindness that forgives me, and I strive to forgive as I am forgiven. I choose to walk the way of lovingkindness with God's gifts of
creation, forgiveness, and reconciliation.

EIGHT

Doing All the Good We Can

The person of the Trinity with whom John Wesley associates perfecting and sanctifying grace is the Spirit. We can choose to deny the movement of the Spirit in our lives. We can ignore the Spirit's nudge toward shalom or the Spirit's offer of zoa. We can pretend we create our own well-being. We are the horse who has been led to water, but we are not forced to drink. We are the woman at the well offered living water,[1] but it is up to us to choose whether we drink and live, or thirst and perish.

The Spirit can appear as good luck, serendipity, or synchronicity. The Spirit's healing might be the word of a friend or stranger. It might be a Bible passage or something in another book. The Spirit might come to us as the needed doctor, the needed podcast, the needed music, the needed sunset, the needed dream, the needed insight, the needed patience, the needed cuddle, the needed still small voice that will heal what is broken and lead us to be the serving love we are made to be.

Wesley encourages that our response to the Spirit be cooperation. Cooperation with the Spirit maximizes our being made more loving and our being used for the purposes of lovingkindness. But what is cooperation with the Spirit? How do we cooperate with "the wind that blows where it will"?[2] Wesley had three guiding principles for cooperating with the Spirit:

Do no harm.

---

1 John 4:1–15.
2 John 3:8.

Do all the good you can.

Practice being with the Spirit.[3]

For the remainder of this chapter, we will consider "Do no harm" and "Do all the good you can." We will consider "Practice being with the Spirit" in the next chapter.

There are many ways to understand "harm" and "good." In therapeutic salvation, "harm" and "good" are defined in the context of lovingkindness creating well-being. Harm is anything that lessens the well-being of an individual and/or community. Good is whatever increases the well-being of an individual and/or community. Harm is that which is not of lovingkindness and good is that which is of lovingkindness. Doing no harm is a way of doing all the good you can. Doing all the good you can is a way of doing no harm.

A favorite quote attributed to John Wesley is, "Do all the good you can, by all the means you can, in all the ways you can, in all the places you can, at all the times you can, to all the people you can, as long as ever you can." It has even been put to music that we might more easily remember.

Discerning harm from good can be difficult. Something as common as breakfast demonstrates the challenges. When shopping for breakfast, we are choosing between doing harm and doing good. We choose the food we eat from a particular manufacturer, who chooses from a set of farmers, who each treat their employees, animals, and land differently. We do all the good we can by supporting manufacturers and producers who care for the well-being of their employees, their livestock, and their land. The well-being of employees includes safe working conditions, adequate pay, and health benefits. For meat and dairy, doing good is supporting producers that care for their fish,

---

3   The method of Methodism is but one way among many to have a relationship with the Spirit. Not being a Methodist or following the Methodist principles or rules is a personal choice and has nothing to do with God's love for any individual. Wesley's rules are meant to judge no one, but they may guide a few. These rules have been of significant guidance to me, offering structure to my being healed for lovingkindness. Those who do not find these rules useful are encouraged to organize their spiritual life in a manner suitable to growing in lovingkindness and in being instruments of lovingkindness.

chickens, pigs, and cattle with lovingkindness. For grain, doing good is supporting those who manage the land with lovingkindness for its well-being. Doing harm is buying coffee from those who mistreat the farmer or worker, who pay little for their labor, and who abuse the land on which the coffee is grown. There are also concerns for our well-being. Does the food we buy have added hormones, pesticides, preservatives, and sugars that can harm us? When making our choices, do we consider how the varying carbon footprints of meat, dairy, and grain do good or harm to the well-being of life on Earth? These are just a few of the choices of harm and good we are called to make before we have breakfast.

My grandfather, a Methodist pastor who served in Oklahoma until his death in 1949, had a list of harms for his children and parishioners to avoid that included smoking, drinking alcohol, card games of any kind, theater, movies, dancing, kissing, cussing, lying, and stealing. When you honored the list, you were doing no harm. Times have changed. Smoking is obviously harmful to our well-being and that of others. Some folks can drink alcohol or smoke dope without harming themselves or others. I can't. Some of us can gamble without harm. I don't because I am too cheap, I don't enjoy having the odds stacked against me, and I will not support an industry that offers a few random rewards while robbing people. However, casinos have become a major economic resource for indigenous people whose land was stolen from them, so maybe I could support a casino to do good for indigenous peoples. There is a long list of harm-causing "isms" in which I sometimes knowingly and sometimes unknowingly participate. Sexism, ageism, racism, educational elitism, and economic privilege are a few. I have phobias of those unlike me that are built into the deep parts of my evolution, psyche, social systems, and culture.

Our imperfections, our desire for low cost and convenience, and our ignorance, both honest and willful, can cause harm. Sometimes doing harm is telling the truth, and sometimes harm is withholding the truth. Sometimes to do good it is necessary to break a law. The situational aspect of harm and good challenges us in our desire to act for the well-being of creation. To do no harm I need a great deal of help from loving friends, mentors, and the Spirit, lived in an ever-flowing stream of forgiveness.

Doing all the good you can, like doing no harm, is concerned both with individuals and with the social order. Doing all the good they could, the early Christians visited the sick, clothed the naked, rescued children from garbage heaps, and shared their wealth generously for the well-being of the community. In eighteenth-century England, there was no public education and no child-protection laws. Children worked at poverty wages in factories and mines. Doing all the good they could, early Methodists created the first Sunday schools, not primarily for religious education, but to teach the three Rs to children trapped in poverty. Doing all the good they could, they addressed the working conditions of industrial labor, including child labor. John Wesley and the British Methodists saw slavery as physical, mental, and spiritual harm to the enslaved and the slaver, to individuals and to the nation. Therefore, in Great Britain, you could not be a Methodist and participate in the harm of slavery. But doing no harm was not enough. The British Methodists did all the good they could by becoming a significant force to end the British slave trade.

Early Methodists were also concerned with the harm that differences of religious belief can and did cause. They lived in a time when religious persecution was frequent and public. There were those stoned and executed because their beliefs differed from others. The stoning of many a Methodist preacher was often organized by the local priest from the Church of England. Here also Methodists tried to do no harm while seeking to do all the good they could, in advocating for religious tolerance. John Wesley lived the differences in his friendship with George Whitefield. Whitefield was a founder with John and Charles Wesley of Methodism and a Calvinistic Methodist pastor. Whitefield led the Evangelical Revival of Great Britain. He developed and successfully practiced open-air preaching, by which he drew a following of thousands to venues outside of church buildings to hear the Gospel. He began open-air preaching because many churches closed their doors to his methods and his message. In 1739, Whitefield decided to take his open-air preaching and revival to Georgia, where he became a leader of the "Great Awakening" in the colonies and a primary leader among Presbyterians. He turned over his Great Britain revival to John Wesley.

John and George did not agree on a person's ability to choose faith versus a person's predestination to be chosen by faith. Wesley strongly held for choice, Whitefield for predestination. In 1741, the differences caused a rift between them that divided their ministries and nearly ended their friendship. Except it didn't end their friendship. When Whitefield died in Massachusetts, a memorial was held in London with John Wesley, at Whitefield's request, officiating. Despite their fundamental theological difference, Whitefield and Wesley worked together for the love of God and the good of the people. For Wesley and Whitefield, "do no harm" was maintaining a relationship. Doing all the good you can was working together for the common good, the well-being of all. In our religiously and politically polarized families, nation, and world, we would do well to remember the universal Spirit of lovingkindness.

Knowing what is harm and what is good and then acting against harm and for good remains a challenge to us and is divisive among us once we leave the breakfast table. In our early colonies, Methodists' adherence to doing no harm and doing all the good they could wavered. Some colonial Methodists were abolitionists, yet others, pastors and bishops included, enslaved people. There were Methodists who voluntarily walked the Trail of Tears with their indigenous brothers and sisters while other Methodists believed and practiced "the only good Indian is a dead Indian." As we consider a woman's right over the control of her body, as we discuss gun laws and mass killings, as we struggle with the human rights issues that exist for people of color and for the LGBTQ+ community, we must question our participation in harm and good. To cooperate with the Spirit is to ask ourselves, "Will this cause harm?" We, of course, don't ultimately know the answer. To cooperate with the Spirit is to ask ourselves, "Will this do all the good I can do?" Again, we don't know the answer. But still, we must act from our best judgment and with the guidance of a loving community and the Spirit.

Systemic racism is particularly on my mind these days as a source of harm. I understand how my white European family history and heritage gained and maintained its privileges by using violence against indigenous and enslaved peoples. In my limited knowledge of my nation's history, its cultural and legal systems of racism, I see harm passed from generation to generation. I am deeply disturbed as I realize how white male privilege is mine at a great expense to others. I, as a white, educated, middle-class male, am the beneficiary of systemic bias in education, career, health care, wealth, shopping (no one follows this old white guy around the store to catch him if he shoplifts), the legal system, and protesting. My white male privilege translates into disenfranchisement, white supremacy, systemic injustice, and violence against people of color. As I strive to be anti-racist, to do no harm, I also struggle with how to leverage my privilege to do all the good I can. I have no easy answers; I try to do what good I can where I am with what I have, trying to give my power and privilege to the oppressed.

When we do all the good we can where and with whom we live, we do justice for the whole of creation. I cannot do everything that needs to be done for lovingkindness, but I can work in lovingkindness for the well-being of the life I touch. I can avoid harm and do good with my children, grandchildren, friends, and congregation, and wherever the Spirit lands me. I can walk with brothers and sisters demanding their human rights. I can't make all the difference, but I can make a difference for lovingkindness in the time and place of my here and now.

By asking the questions of harm and good, we are forced to stop and evaluate our thoughts and actions. By pausing to evaluate what is harm and what is good, we open ourselves to perfecting and sanctifying grace; we present ourselves to be made more loving, that we might be instruments of well-being for the cosmos. In radical dependence on forgiving and reconciling grace, we do our best to embody lovingkindness by doing no harm while doing all the good we can.

NINE

Practice Being with the Spirit

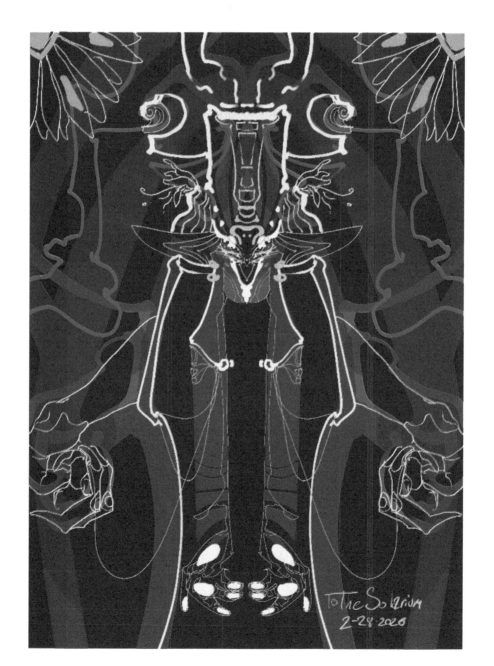

During my first few years of following in the way of Jesus, I was a mediocre disciple. I went to worship because I was expected to show up. I studied scripture because it was fascinating. My prayer life was sporadic. I didn't fast or abstain. I was only in classes that were required or that I led.

While meditating during a silent retreat, an image came to me of Jesus teaching a small crowd. The crowd was leaning in, listening, learning, being transformed. I saw myself standing at the back of the crowd, not quite a part of them, and ready to leave should something uncomfortable happen. I had a passion for God's love and justice but was not fully engaged or committed to any community or method that might heal my failures and perfect me in lovingkindness. Yet even in my tepid following, the Spirit persisted and nurtured me.

Spiritual practice is the practice of being loving and kind that we might be better at lovingkindness, that lovingkindness might become a habit, might be our most common way of being. One of the gifts to me from Celtic Christianity is the concept of "thin places." Thin places are places and times we easily experience the Spirit, where our spirit and the Spirit are close, places where we are warmed by lovingkindness. Thin places can be geographical, situational, and relational. Doing no harm and doing all the good we can are thin places. Through them we experience being lovingkindness in cooperation with the Spirit and we open ourselves to the transformation offered by the Spirit. The Spirit is, of course, everywhere always. But some places, times, rituals, and circumstances seem to be particularly thin. Choosing to be in thin places is choosing to practice being with the Spirit. By this practice, the Spirit has greater opportunity to heal and use us, perfect and sanctify us, reducing the harm in us created by our failures to be lovingkindness, increasing the lovingkindness in us that we more often do good. When we are cooperative and attentive to our spiritual practices, the Spirit heals us in ways we are unable to do by our own will and heals the deeply broken parts of us hidden in our unconscious.

Practice is repetition for improvement. When practicing a musical instrument, we practice both in private and with an orchestra or band. If we are to improve on our instrument, both private and communal practice are essential. Like practicing a musical instrument, spiritual practices have both private and communal thin places. Enduring faith families, such as Christianity, Judaism, Hinduism, Buddhism, and Islam, have traditional methods or practices for staying in touch with the Spirit, and these can be guides to us. In Judaism and Christianity, the traditional thin places are worship, prayer, study, and fasting; and each has both a private and communal aspect.

Worship

The most common Greek word translated as "worship" and "adoration" in the Christian scriptures is a form of *proskuneo.* "Proskuneo" is an active verb meaning "to kiss toward." To worship and adore, in the Middle Eastern tradition, is to lie prostrate before the master, maybe kiss the master's feet or hand, with a readiness to do the master's will. We humans are not so good at proskuneo. The dogs that have adopted me have been great at proskuneo. To lie prostrate before another is humbling, even humiliating. To be unquestioningly obedient is difficult.

Worshipful adoration is not something to be done lightly because not all masters are worthy of absolute adoration. I do not proskuneo before the punitive king. I do not lie prostrate before rules and laws interpreted and reinterpreted by a selective elite to be imposed on others. A God whose primary task is to mete out Heaven or Hell based on divine rules applied to a suffering creation is not the God I "kiss toward."

But I eagerly worship, adore, and prostrate myself before the God who is lovingkindness. To worship and adore the God revealed in agape is to choose to be open to, be obedient to, and cooperate with the lovingkindness that flows through the universe. I do not control that flow, but I can choose to enter its movement and be taken where its desire will take me. I privately practice worship at a small altar in my home because I need a concrete place with symbols of love. On my altar, I have a candle, sweetgrass and sage, a redtail hawk and an eagle feather, an abalone shell, Psalm 131, some prayers, and a cross. Nearby are a few Bibles, a book of daily devotions, and a Russian Orthodox iconographic painting signifying lovingkindness. I have rocks from holy sites I have visited. I have pictures of people who love me. At my altar I am immersed in lovingkindness.

I also practice worship with a community who imperfectly worship the God who is lovingkindness. I pray with them, sing with them, hear scripture with them, and am silent with them. I need to drink the wine and taste the bread of Holy Communion. I need to renew the vows of my baptism and the promise to love and care for every child of God. In communal worship, I publicly renew my commitment to be a living offering to lovingkindness for the transformation of the world.

Prayer

Prayer for me is an aligning of my mind, heart, soul, and strength with the Spirit. There is much written on prayer by great and wise people. Jesus had advice about prayer and taught his disciples to pray.[1] Henri Nouwen and Thomas Merton offer deep wisdom on prayer.[2] Evelyn Underhill has been a prayer guide.[3] Thich Nhat Hanh's mindful meditation is prayer for me.[4] For guidance, you are better off looking to these people than to me.

I try to pray daily at my home altar, several times throughout the day as I find occasion, before I go to sleep at night, and at least weekly

---

1   Matthew 6:5–15, 7:7–11; Luke 11:1–4.

2   Henri Nouwen, *The Way of the Heart Connecting with God through Prayer, Wisdom, and Silence* (San Francisco: HarperOne, 1991). Thomas Merton, *Contemplative Prayer* (New York: Herder and Herder, 1969).

3   Evelyn Underhill, *Practical Mysticism: A Little Book for Normal People* (Radford, VA: Wilder Publications, 2018).

4   Thich Nhat Hanh, *The Miracle of Mindfulness: An Introduction to the Miracle of Mindfulness* (Boston: Beacon Press, 1975).

with my faith community. The prayers of my childhood were usually self-serving, asking God for gifts or help. The process theologian John Cobb helped me understand that God already knows my needs and those of the world.[5] God knows, before I know, who is sick, who is suffering, and where the disaster just happened, and God is already acting for healing. When I pray for someone's health or situation, I now pray, "God, I join my love to Yours for the well-being of _____." I choose in intercessory prayer to partner my spirit with God's Spirit for the best that can be where the world suffers. I have come to believe that joining my spirit with the Spirit effects change for well-being beyond what I am able to physically accomplish. In this way I partner with God in body and spirit for the well-being of all.

Also important to me are my prayers of supplication, of surrender. At my altar in the morning and before I go to sleep at night, I give myself to the Spirit, to be healed by the Spirit and directed by the Spirit. My prayers of surrender have evolved into a silent, meditative listening. I listen not so much for words, though sometimes words come, but for the experience of being held in and guided by the Spirit's lovingkindness. I could go to a thousand thin places, practicing all the traditional spiritual habits every day, but without surrender to the Spirit I remain the same old grump. To be healed by the Spirit I must not only choose to show up, but I must also choose to open up. As a supplicant I surrender my life to an uncertain and undefined future shaped by the Spirit of lovingkindness.

Surrendering control and submitting to the Spirit is not easy for me. The standard final asana of yoga is the sponge or corpse pose. In the corpse pose, one lies faceup and spread-eagle, breathing rhythmically while opening every cell in the body to the energy of the universe, the Spirit. When I began this practice in 1972, I simply rested in the corpse pose, having completed the other asanas. A decade later, I realized that if I were to fully practice the corpse, I had to release control of

---

5   John Cobb, *Praying for Jennifer: An Exploration of Intercessory Prayer in Story Form* (Nashville: The Upper Room, 1985).

my mind and body. However, I was afraid that if I did so I would die. So I did partial releases, ready to snatch my spirit back from the Spirit should things head in a direction that frightened me. Two years later, I realized that a tentative release meant I was still in control, so I took deep breaths, and let go of my life. I practiced trusting the Spirit even though I was still afraid I might die. It took twelve years of being the corpse to come to this simple understanding. Releasing control of my body, mind, and spirit to the Spirit continues to be a challenging and maturing process for me.

Regular communal prayer happens at meals in our house when we thank God for daily bread, daily life, and daily love. It is a simple daily act of joining with others in offering prayerful gratitude to God. I join in communal prayer at weekly worship where I pray the Lord's Prayer, pray for the well-being of individuals, for my family and community, for all those who suffer, and for the world. In worship we sing the prayers of our faith. There is a healing power in being with a group of folks who trust that God is listening deeply to their lives and continually reaching to us in lovingkindness with the gifts of creation, forgiveness, and healing.

Study

Study has been and remains a great gift in my being with the Spirit. I study the Bible almost daily because it is the witness of my faith family. I am not a biblical literalist. I see how the Bible's composition is filled with human error and failings. There are images of God in the Bible that confuse me and some that I reject. There are rules in the Bible that I will not keep—see appendix 4. But even so, I see shining through all the Bible's human frailty the Spirit of love, compassion, kindness, and justice.

I love to read books about the Bible and faith. I am aware of how my personal bias and inadequacies can skew my study. My private study benefits from and needs to be pursued in community. I read

Bible commentaries and theological works from a variety of perspectives and faiths. I place myself in classes with others who are also seeking to cooperate with the Spirit and grow in lovingkindness.

I love books in general; they are windows and doors into amazing worlds. It was Nikos Kazantzakis' *The Last Temptation of Christ* that moved me to want to be loving like Jesus. Books on the brain, history, psychology, and sociology, biographies, and novels open me to the Spirit. I find no conflict between faith and science. Science helps me understand how creation functions. Faith teaches me why creation functions. Study helps me understand what it means to be me and us, opens me to new thoughts and ways, and makes room for the Spirit to blow into my mind.

John Wesley once said, "Reading Christians are growing Christians. When Christians cease to read, they cease to grow." The mind is a gift from God. Our ability to learn, listen to the learning of others, and share our learning makes progressive transformation for individuals and societies possible. When we cease using our minds, we get lost and wander down peculiar and dangerous wormholes.

Fasting and Abstinence

Many of the early Methodists fasted after Thursday supper until Friday supper, missing two meals. It was a practice of cooperation with the Spirit. They gave the money they saved to feed the hungry. In our consumptive culture, fasting and abstinence are much neglected. There are multiple occasions when fasting and abstinence, by the power of the Spirit, have transformed me into a more loving person.

From childhood, I, and those around me, suffered from my explosive temper. From an early age, I wanted to be free and to free others from my rage. I repeatedly tried self-will as the cure, but it never worked. During the healing service of the Cursillo I attended in 1984, I prayed with the spiritual director that I be healed of my rage. I didn't know what would happen next, I just knew I needed healing because I was harming my family. Following the healing prayer, an idea popped into my head, an idea I took to be from the Spirit. After a rage event, I was to fast for three days, drinking only water or juice, and to pray for the Spirit to heal me. I explained to Vickie and our daughters, ages five and seven, what I was doing and why. While fasting I would sit with them during mealtime but not eat. At one of the meals at which I was fasting, our five-year-old decided not to eat. We asked her why. She said she was quicking. Fast and quick were confused in her mind, and that was cute. What brought awe was when I realized she was fasting with me for my healing. She wanted to help me be healed. Within two months and three fasts, I no longer had rage events. The Spirit changed me. I don't understand nor can I explain why fasting worked. And I don't know if it will work for everyone. Let the Spirit guide you.

Sometime around 1990, I recognized a deep fear in myself. It felt like a knot below my stomach. I began numbing that fear with alcohol. I was not a steady drinker but increasingly a binge drinker. My family history told me that should I continue, I would do harm to my family and to my ministry. On July 13, 1993, I quit drinking, and on July 17, I attended my first Alcoholics Anonymous meeting. The AA group laughed when I said I thought I might be an alcoholic because they knew, and I didn't know, that since I thought I might be an alcoholic, I probably was an alcoholic. They had been there and done that. I attended meetings regularly, got a sponsor, read the Big Book, and began working the twelve steps. The Spirit in the AA community gave me strength not to drink, and my fear was replaced with serenity. The fears of failing as a husband, father, pastor, and person were mostly gone. The fear of being exposed as a fraud, the fear that led me to lie about stupid stuff, the constant comparison of myself to others, was generally replaced with a peaceful quietness. I could be an honest, open, authentic me. I continue to abstain from alcohol and to be a recovering alcoholic. I still get afraid, but I don't live in fear. I am free to be forgiven when I fail and to forgive when I am betrayed. Thanks to the Spirit in AA, I remain sober and mostly serene.

Another gift of fasting is the act of joining our spirit in solidarity with those who hunger and thirst, with the oppressed and despised. Fasting in solidarity with the oppressed is a choice we can make. I am fortunate enough that I can stop a fast by going to the pantry. Most in the world have no pantry, not even a bread box. I believe that joining my spirit with the Spirit's lovingkindness for the benefit of the vulnerable and oppressed transforms me into an instrument God uses to transform injustice to justice, war to peace, and chaos to well-being for the world.

I have over time also learned that it is sometimes necessary to abstain from relationships that do more harm than good. The harm can be physical, emotional, or spiritual. Some of us are toxic for some others. Those who are codependent or abused in a relationship must end the relationship if a healing transformation is not clearly evidenced. The easiest signal that someone is toxic for me is when the relationship leads away from doing good and toward doing harm. A member of a congregation I served asked me to visit and pray with an acquaintance of hers. I made contact, arranged a time, and went to the acquaintance's home. On the first visit I was hopeful I might aid in her well-being and arranged to visit once a month. On the second visit I saw no desire in her to change and felt my visit accomplished nothing. After five visits I felt depressed. Being in her presence was being in the presence of an emotional black hole that sucked the life out of me. I increasingly carried her gloom into other relationships. She was toxic for me. I ended the visits, praying that the Spirit send her someone who could help her.

Fasting is no longer a choice for me because the medications I take require food to be effective. Going off the meds has deadly consequences. I miss fasting. I miss its spiritual uplift and healing. If you are physically able to fast, to unite your spirit with the Spirit for your transformation to lovingkindness and for the transformation of the world to lovingkindness, then I encourage you to do so.

Spiritual Conferencing

Spiritual conferencing was added by John Wesley to the more traditional practices. Wesley divided the early Methodists into small groups of ten to twelve people. Each group met weekly with an assigned leader. Wesley directed that each member of a group was to be held accountable by the group for doing no harm, doing all the good they could, and their regular practice of being with the Spirit. Spiritual conferencing is this flawed self hanging out with other flawed selves who want to be less flawed. It is the practice that holds us accountable to an integrity of talk and walk.

In AA, we have a home group and a sponsor to hold us accountable for the steps of our recovery. The group and the sponsor are no less flawed than each of us, but when the members of the group speak of their experience, strength, and hope, we are reminded of our experience, strength, and hope. My sponsor is given permission to call me on my BS when I am blindly in denial, and to encourage me when I feel hopeless. Though I often don't like being held accountable, I admit that the group is often wiser than I am. Listening for group wisdom above my own opinion, the thought of being accountable to someone else for my actions has often caused me to think more carefully and sometimes to change my opinion and behavior. Like those watching their weight or engaging in an exercise program, being held accountable by a group increases the probability of success.

We modern humans don't like being held accountable. The ever-strengthening concept of individualism places emphasis upon "doing it my way" and "my freedom," both of which eschew communal accountability. We live in a culture in which even spirituality, and perhaps especially spirituality, has been thought of as personal and no one else's business. Consequently, there are so-called spiritual folks who, in their fierce and righteous individualism, do harm to themselves and are toxic to others. The practice of spiritual conferencing with those who seek to love God, neighbor, and self is an essential corrective to toxic social and spiritual individualism. I am the one responsible for the choices I make, but being held accountable to the group for those choices makes me more loving. Showing up with people who want to live and love better has helped me live and love better.

Personal Disciplines

There are many thin places other than traditional worship, study, prayer, fasting, and spiritual conferencing. Each of us is asked to discover our own best thin places for lovingkindness. These are the places we feel close to the love of God and the uplifting of the Spirit. These thin places can be formative memories, persons of deep love, weddings, funerals, books, and conversations. For many, music and art are thin places. For others, being in nature is a thin place. I have countless thin places. Holding hands and a good-night kiss with Vickie are thin places. A meal with my family is a thin place. Backpacking is a thin place. Sailing is a thin place. Being near water is a thin place. Silence is a thin place. Children and grandchildren are thin places. Surprisingly, suffering can be a thin place. Sitting with the dying, listening to another's struggles, failing as a pastor, having cancer, are all places that have led me to lovingkindness. I know that for many, suffering as a thin place is counterintuitive, since we live in a culture that prefers to avoid and deny both suffering and death. I hope that my later explanation of the joy of "a peace that passes understanding" will help.

What is essential to our well-being is for each of us to know and visit the traditional and personal thin places of our lives. When with intentionality and regularity we visit the Spirit in thin places, we cooperate with the Spirit's transformative power. Our cooperation with the Spirit opens us to being transformed into lovingkindness. Visiting the Spirit in thin places increases the probability that we will be used for lovingkindness. The spiritual practice of being with the Spirit, of cooperating with the Spirit, and of being available to be used by the

Spirit is a choice we can make for our well-being, the well-being of our relationships, and the well-being of creation.

A life lived in lovingkindness is both loving God by being with the Spirit and loving our neighbor as ourselves by doing all the good we can. In Wesleyan spirituality, both being with the Spirit and loving our neighbor as ourselves are of equal emphasis. Being in the thin places and acting in lovingkindness are meant to be lived simultaneously and harmoniously. Too often, loving God and loving our neighbor as ourselves are separated. It seems difficult for humans to keep two things in their mind at the same time. Sometimes the practice of being with lovingkindness and the practice of doing lovingkindness are treated as if one is more valuable or more important than the other, or as if one needs to precede the other. However, without each in balance, they falter and fail.

For example, recently the United Methodist Church has made doing lovingkindness a major concern and neglected the personal and corporate of practices of being with lovingkindness. Though active in the effort to feed the hungry and clothe the naked, many United Methodists don't worship regularly, don't study the Bible, don't pray regularly, don't fast, and don't hold themselves accountable to others for their spiritual practices. But it wasn't that long ago that United Methodists focused on the practices of being with the Spirit and neglected doing lovingkindness. So, while being regular at worship and knowing their Bible, many were indifferent or resistant to doing lovingkindness on issues such as war, racism, misogyny, equitable health care, and the poor. When being with lovingkindness and doing lovingkindness are divided, and sometimes placed in competition, then both suffer, and the healing of the Spirit for individuals, community, and all creation is impeded.

In Sunburst, Montana, there was no hospital and no doctor. The nearest medical services were twenty-eight miles south in Shelby. A volunteer ambulance crew served Sunburst and the North Toole County area of about six hundred people spread over one thousand square miles. The ambulance was vital to the community. I was recruited by a member of the congregation to train as an emergency medical technician and to ride in the ambulance. For three years I served as an EMT on the Sunburst ambulance. One Sunday, my three-year-old daughter and I were in Sweetgrass, and my ambulance pager went off during worship. A trucker around the corner from the church needed an ambulance. I was the nearest EMT. I had to choose between finishing worship or leaving worship and my daughter to go to the aid of a stranger. I looked out at the congregation and asked, "Should I go?" From the back pew, Jeanette McAlpine, a tough sheep rancher, shouted, "If it was me, you damn well better get there!" I went to the aid of the trucker while those in worship cared for my daughter and went to the fellowship hall for coffee. Once the trucker was stable, safely in the ambulance, and on his way with the rest of the ambulance crew to the hospital, I returned to the church, and we continued to worship. Being with the Spirit and doing lovingkindness were in balance.

A pastor of another congregation also trained and volunteered for the ambulance. We had different faith understandings, and while we were on ambulance runs, we would engage in a theological or a biblical discussion. I am a sucker for a good debate because it is a form of study. I slowly realized that the discussions caused us to neglect those we were serving, that I was engaged in study when I was supposed to be doing lovingkindness. I told the other pastor that I needed to stop our discussions while on ambulance runs and focus on the well-being of those we were serving. I needed to keep the practices of cooperating with the Spirit and doing all the good I could in their right places. When in balance, the practice of being with lovingkindness and doing lovingkindness guide us and transform us to living the way of lovingkindness.

Faith, Hope, Lovingkindness, and Joy

I am not a fatalist—what will be will be; nor a determinist—the future is fixed. I am confident that the choices we make influence the future we experience. I believe that we can choose to be grateful, accept forgiveness, and practice cooperating with the Spirit. I trust that when we choose the way of lovingkindness, the Spirit works with us to perfect us in being lovingkindness and guides us to serve with lovingkindness. My elevator speech runs like this:

> God is lovingkindness. Made in the image of God, I am lovingkindness. Sadly, I sometimes fail to be lovingkindness. God forgives me. The Spirit of God heals me and uses me for lovingkindness. Lovingkindness grows in me faith, hope, and joy, and I am made a partner with God for the well-being of the cosmos.

Following the way of lovingkindness is challenging because life is challenging. My wife and I have health issues. Not all my relationships are what I hope they might be. The United Methodist Church, my church, has areas in which lovingkindness is being failed. My social and political communities are suffering vitriolic division. The damage we are doing to our planet, and thus to ourselves, is collective insanity. We are made to be and do better than this. I see lovingkindness offering a way forward to healing, to our salvation. When Paul writes his poem on the character of lovingkindness to the church in Corinth, he ends it with "faith, hope, and lovingkindness persevere, these three; but the greatest of these is lovingkindness."[1] Faith, hope, and lovingkindness define, for Paul, the character, actions, and life of those who follow the way of Jesus.

Faith

The Greek word from Christian scriptures translated as faith is *pistis*. It is a word with a diversity and depth of meaning. Its cluster of synonyms

---

1   1 Corinthians 13:13.

includes "belief," "trust," "faith," "honesty," "confidence," and "assurance." I focus on three related concepts: faith as belief, faith as trust, and faith as confidence. These are not three different understandings of faith but are three facets of a single expression.

Faith understood as belief is a cognitive decision often based upon a person's reasoning or the command of an external authority. When someone tells me something, I believe it is true or I believe it is not true. I have faith in their word, or I don't have faith in their word. In the context of spirituality, I can believe a creedal statement or not. I can believe there is Spirit or not. Belief is an activity of my reasoning something to be true or to be not true. Faith as cognitive belief is most often based on what an individual perceives as reasonable, or what a group accepts as reasonable, and the foundation of a worldview by which to operate.

Faith is also trust. Trust is not a cognitive activity of choice, but an emotional response developed over time. I trust someone whom I have experienced as trustworthy, and I don't trust those whom I have experienced as untrustworthy. I trust a particular statement because it has been reliable or distrust it because it has failed me. Trust is not chosen but experienced and needs shared life and time to grow. I can choose to act in trust, but that is not the same as trusting. Whereas belief is an operation of the mind, trust is an operation of the emotions, of the heart.

Faith is also confidence. Confidence is a Latin compound word. It joins *con to fide*, "with" joined to "faith." When I believe someone and trust someone, I approach them with faith. I am confident that with them I am safe. An example might help here. As I write this, Vickie is my wife of fifty years. When we first fell in love and Vickie said, "I love you," I believed her because I chose and wanted to believe her. It had taken two months for me to get a date with her. We dated only one month before we were engaged. A mere three months after that, we were married. Over the years of perfecting our relationship, raising children, pursuing careers, and experiencing hard times in body, mind, and soul, I have come to trust Vickie. My trusting her was not a choice but the result of time together; it was not a product of my frontal lobes but of my experience, over time, of emotional security with her. Believing Vickie and trusting Vickie led me to being confident, a life stance of looking forward with faith, that life with Vickie will be one of fulfillment, joy, and well-being, both in the easy and in the hard times. I believe Vickie, I trust Vickie, and I am confident in the future of our relationship.

I have to offer an aside here. It has to do with my hamartia, my missing the mark, which impedes faith. I am not yet complete in lovingkindness, and therefore any relationship I have is imperfect. Also, I suffer from a fear of abandonment. That means after fifty years of marriage I am sometimes still frightened Vickie will leave me. This is related to my fear of being inadequate for love, which leads to thinking that there are others who might make her happier, that there could be better people in the world for her, that I am not good enough for her, that I am unable to accept fully the forgiveness she offers, and that I am unable to forgive myself when I fail to love her rightly. My fear leads me to try and control Vickie and our relationship. Those who have gotten this far in the book will recognize that this has nothing to do with Vickie's faithfulness but is my own failure, my sin. I am graced that Vickie's love and the Spirit's kindness have been a constant in perfecting me and moving me closer to complete belief, trust, and confidence in our relationship.

Faith in God also follows the threefold understanding of belief, trust, and confidence. To believe in God is to believe there is a higher power. Each of us has our own understanding of a higher power. I understand the manifestation of that higher power to be the gifts and fruits of lovingkindness in creation, forgiveness, and healing. I choose to believe God is lovingkindness and lovingkindness is God. Faith in God is also my experience of being in relationship with an ineffable and uncontrollable lovingkindness over time. The time of believing in God has grown trust in me so that I can be vulnerable and risk being grateful, accepting, and cooperative. My trusting in lovingkindness deepens with experience. Faith in God, both as belief and trust, has grown my confidence in lovingkindness. I anticipate that in the best of times I will be held steady or humbled appropriately. I am confident that in the worst of times I will be able to rest "in a peace that passes understanding."[2] Confidence in lovingkindness can be easy in the good times. It is in the difficult times that such confidence is hard to explain though often deepened. If I could explain how suffering grows faith, I would do so, but I don't have an explanation for this strange phenomenon. I can only witness that the most difficult times of my life have been an impetus for my faith in lovingkindness to grow stronger, firmer, and more trusted by me. As I practice being in the thin places, I discover and become confident that, in fact, all places and all times are thin places of lovingkindness, even dank and ugly places. I discover that every part of life is filled with grace. I come to anticipate that every sunset is the most beautiful. I begin to expect that every tragedy offers a gift of lovingkindness.

Now that I have tried to make faith tidy and sequential, I admit that it is not this way in my experience. Sometimes I trust, as I did with Vickie, before I believe. I find that I am strangely confident when I have no solid reason for belief and no experience over time of trust. The Spirit is weird that way. For me, this is true: Doing no harm, doing all the good I can, and practicing being with the Spirit has grown in me a firmer belief, a deeper trust, and a more confident faith, but not necessarily in that order.

There is a downside to growing in faith. As awareness of lovingkindness is sharpened, our encounters with failures to be lovingkindness become increasingly painful because we know we are better than our failures. It is more painful for us when a relationship falters, a politic polarizes, and the Earth screams of her dying. When we watch the news, we sometimes think and feel that the world is a place of unending waste and violence. There is also an upside to our

---

2 Philippians 4:7.

awakening to lovingkindness. For something to be news, it must be out of the ordinary. News is "man bites dog," not "dog bites man." News is "wife shot husband," not "wife kissed husband." The news tells us where lovingkindness has failed. But each failure on the news is an exception, the unusual moment, to the billions of times lovingkindness has succeeded. In the news we don't hear of the daily lovingkindness of spouses and parents, of friends and neighbors. In the news we don't hear of the strangers who gave aid at great risk. In the news we miss those who search with diligence for a lost child, for a cure to cancer, for a way to house and feed the poor, at significant cost to their own lives. To awaken to lovingkindness, to live in lovingkindness, to have our lives restored to lovingkindness, leads us to see how all around us is the continual wonder of lovingkindness lived in small and large ways. Over time, we grow more aware of the constant presence of lovingkindness in all creation, and with faith, we confidently rejoice to be alive in such a world as ours.

Hope

Most of Christian scripture uses *elpis* when speaking of hope. "Elpis" is a simple word that can be translated as both "hope" and "expectation." When one cooperates with the Spirit, there grows a positive expectation of the future. Spiritual hope is not naïve hope, nor a hope that ignores cruelty, suffering, or death. It is a realistic hope that looks to the future, expecting lovingkindness to prevail, if not today, then someday.

The Montana Logging and Ballet Company, who neither log nor plié but are from Montana, is a group of four satirical musicians and actors. They gave me a phrase that rings true for describing realistic hope. In their song "Love Is the Journey," by Steve Garnaas-Holmes, they sing of the "unexpected ending of a story." Hope is when we come to expect lovingkindness to be the unexpected ending to a story. That is, when we cannot see a way to a better outcome, we still expect and watch for a better way to come. When in desperation I went on the

Benedictine silent retreats, I went because I was suffering and saw no way out of the suffering. After the first retreat, I began to expect an unexpected gift of healing and direction every time I went, and I was never disappointed. These retreats became an annual way of practicing being with the Spirit, and expecting the unexpected became a spiritual habit.

A congregation I was sent to serve was near bankruptcy, and I had no ideas on how we might stop the financial bleeding. I was sitting hopeless in my car in an empty parking lot after a particularly dire administrative board meeting, and I prayed. I felt the Spirit say, "These people have everything they need." From that moment I began to expect the unexpected, and for reasons completely outside my control the debt was paid within five years. I believe it is realistic hope to expect God to surprise me with unexpected grace.

Martin Seligman is a research psychologist. His research on learned helplessness and learned optimism helps me better understand realistic hope. Seligman has demonstrated that under certain conditions dogs and humans become unable to see a path out of the limits of their current situation, even though a clear alternative may be present. When encountering a frustration, those who have learned to be helpless believe they can't do anything about it, and so they don't try. In this condition the person is said to be functioning from learned helplessness.

One day the Spirit acted through a student of Seligman's. The student asked the simple question, "Why do some individuals escape learned helplessness and others do not?" The question transformed Seligman and his research. Seligman subsequently developed his work on learned optimism, which became the basis for most of his later publications. Apparently, some individuals, while accepting their current circumstances, as horrendous as they may be, continue looking for and expecting to find ways in which those circumstances can be improved. When we live in the way of lovingkindness, we are freed of our supposed limitations for well-being and are alert to opportunities to improve our well-being and the well-being of others. We make what changes we can, even if that means protesting, divorce, immigration, a change of career, or any of the many ways humans seek to improve their well-being and the well-being of creation.

Similar advice comes from one of my favorite podcasts, *Hidden Brain*, hosted by Shankar Vedantam. In the episode titled "Minimizing Pain, Maximizing Joy," Vedantam interviews the philosopher William Irvine on the principles of stoicism that can assist us in times of struggle. Irvine offers that stoicism suggests an attitude that faces challenges under the belief that we have power to affect a better, if not the preferred, future. According to Irvine, to be stoic is to do what you can with what you've got, where you are. Reinhold Niebuhr says it well in the Serenity Prayer: "God, grant me the serenity to accept the things I cannot change, the courage to change the things I can, and the wisdom to know the difference." Hope is believing that we have the power to change at least some aspect of a situation toward lovingkindness.

Realistic hope heals learned helplessness by opening our eyes to unexpected potential, and gently moves us to work for our best possible future. We do not control our futures because our future is dependent on a present that is the nexus of multiple circumstances, influenced by the decisions of others, over whom we have no control. However, we do influence our futures with our attitudes, expectations, and efforts. Those who look to the future believing they can make a positive difference are more likely to discover a portion of a kinder future and to live into it. Those who cooperate with the Spirit and grow in lovingkindness grow in hopeful expectation of tomorrow and next year. Such hopeful expectation is the result of expecting lovingkindness in all creation, and the experience of being in lovingkindness over time.

Lovingkindness

Lovingkindness, as both a noun and a verb, names the nature of our being and the purpose of our doing. We begin with lovingkindness as our way of being. Every spiritual tradition has an ethos, a set of moral principles that describes a preferred way of being. Buddhism offers the eightfold path of right understanding, right thought, right speech, right action, right livelihood, right effort, right mindfulness, and right concentration. Around 54 CE, Paul wrote his first letter to the church in Corinth. In that letter he pens a poem about the ethos of lovingkindness.

> If I speak in the languages of humans and of angels, but have not lovingkindness, I am a noisy gong or a clanging cymbal. And if I have prophetic powers, and understand all mysteries and all knowledge, and I have all faith, so as to remove mountains, but have not lovingkindness, I am nothing. If I give away all I have, and if I deliver my body to be destroyed, but have not lovingkindness, I gain nothing.
>
> Lovingkindness is patient and kind; lovingkindness is not malicious or boastful; it is not arrogant or rude. Lovingkindness does not insist on its own way; it is not irritable or resentful; it does not rejoice at wrong but rejoices in the right. Lovingkindness endures all things, believes all things, hopes all things, suffers all things. Lovingkindness never ends.[3]

Paul also identifies the ethos of lovingkindness as the fruit of the Spirit, listing the character qualities nurtured by a life lived in lovingkindness. He writes to the church in Galatia, "The fruit of the Spirit is love, joy, peace, patience, kindness, goodness, faithfulness, gentleness, and self-control."[4] As the Spirit matures us in lovingkindness, these are the character traits we can expect to develop in us.

The way of lovingkindness calls us not only to be lovingkindness but also to act with lovingkindness for God and our neighbor as ourselves. To act with lovingkindness is to serve the well-being of those who need compassion, healing, and justice without asking for

---

3   1 Corinthians 13:1–8.

4   Galatians 5:22–23.

or expecting something in return. I have said Jesus is my teacher and my vision of how lovingkindness speaks and behaves when human. In Luke's Gospel, Jesus began his teaching ministry in his home synagogue in Nazareth. While in worship, he was handed the scroll of Isaiah and he stood to read, "The Spirit of the Lord is upon me, because he has anointed me to preach good news to the poor. He has sent me to proclaim release to the captives and recovering of sight to the blind, to set at liberty those who are oppressed, to proclaim the acceptable year of the Lord."[5] With this reading, Jesus announced his purpose and defines what it means to act in lovingkindness.

My favorite Gospel is that of Mark. A favorite theme of Mark is found in Jesus' teachings of his coming death in a trilogy of stories. Three times Jesus announces his upcoming crucifixion and resurrection, three times the disciples don't understand his purpose, and three times Jesus responds to their error with a teaching on being servants of all. In the first story, after Jesus' announcement, Peter rebukes Jesus for teaching that "the son of man must suffer many things and be rejected." Jesus then rebukes Peter, "Get behind me, Satan! For you are not on the side of God, but of men." Jesus calls together both the crowd and the disciples and teaches servant lovingkindness: "If anyone would follow me, let that one deny their self and take their cross and imitate me. For whoever would save their life will lose it; and whoever loses their life for my sake and the sake of the good news I teach will save it. For what does it profit someone, to gain the whole world and forfeit their life?"[6] Jesus teaches that the way of lovingkindness is the way of giving our lives in service for the well-being of others.

In the second story of the trilogy, Jesus again teaches his disciples of his coming death and resurrection. Again they don't understand what he says, though it seems plain enough, and they are afraid to ask. When they arrive at a house in Capernaum, Jesus asks them what they were talking about on the way. "They were silent; for on the way they

---

5   Luke 4:16–21; Isaiah 61:1–2.

6   Mark 8:31–38.

had discussed with one another who was the greatest." Jesus sits them down and for a second time explains what it means to be great in lovingkindness, saying, "'If anyone would be first, that one must be last of all and servant of all.' And he took a child and put the child in the midst of them; and taking the child in his arms, he said to them, 'Whoever gives hospitality to one such child in my name gives hospitality to me; and whoever is hospitable to me, is hospitable not to me but the one who sent me.'"[7] Children, more than any others, need the hospitality of lovingkindness because they are the least powerful and most vulnerable. The well-being of children is completely dependent upon others. To act in lovingkindness is to take good care of the children. And to take good care of children is to take good care of God.

In the third story, Jesus again teaches his death and resurrection. Immediately following his teaching, the disciples James and John, who are brothers, come to Jesus and say, "Teacher, we want you to do for us whatever we ask of you." It is an audacious request for any student to make of their teacher. Jesus indulges them, saying, "What do you want me to do for you?" They say to him, "Grant us to sit, one at your right hand and one at your left, in your glory." The right and left hand are the positions of greatest power; they signify the master's blessing and authority. Jesus asks if they are able to suffer what he will suffer. They say they are able. Jesus says he is not the one who will decide who sits at his right and left hand. Then he gathers all the disciples and teaches of the servanthood of lovingkindness: "You know that those who are supposed to rule over the Gentiles lord it over them, and their great men exercise authority over them. But it shall not be so among you; whoever would be great among you must be your servant, and whoever would be first among you must be slave of all. For the son of man also came not to be served but to serve, and to give his life for the liberation of many."[8] To be powerful, in the way of Jesus, is not having

---

7   Mark 9:30–36.

8   Mark 10:32–44.

"power over" but is to have "power for" the many. To act in lovingkindness is to act for the well-being of all.

When we choose the way of lovingkindness, our character and our actions will be more often of lovingkindness. Choosing to be grateful, to accept forgiveness, and to cooperate with the Spirit increases God's opportunity to transform our deepest selves to be lovingkindness even as God is lovingkindness.

Joy

To Paul's faith, hope, and lovingkindness, I add joy or happiness. It is my experience and the witness of others that a byproduct of the way of lovingkindness is joy. Joy is not something we create in ourselves but something that comes of its own accord and in its own way. In the way of lovingkindness, joy finds and lifts us. In his sermon "God's Love to Fallen Humankind," John Wesley wrote, "All worldly joys are less than that one joy of doing kindness."[9]

Some of the most beloved verses of the Gospels are the beatitudes found in the Gospels of Matthew and Luke.[10] Matthew's first beatitude, in Jesus' Sermon on the Mount, is "Blessed are the poor in spirit, for theirs is the kingdom of Heaven." "Blessed" is translated from the Greek *makaria* and means "happiness, bliss." And "poor in spirit" is the equivalent of "depressed." So, the first beatitude could read, "Happy are the depressed." On its face, this is contradictory and makes no sense. Then the kingdom of Heaven is offered as if it is a reward for being depressed in the same way a hospital is a reward for being gravely ill. Couldn't we just skip being depressed or ill and get straight to joy? Luke's version is no better. Where Matthew has "the poor in spirit," Luke simply writes, "Blessed are you poor, for yours is the kingdom of God." Again, it is a paradox and could read, "Happy are the poor," who then, somehow, get

---

9   John Wesley, "God's Love to Fallen Humankind," Bible Hub, biblehub.com.
10   Matthew 5:1–11; Luke 6:20–26.

the kingdom of God. How can it be that the depressed and the poor are blissful, happy, and blessed with the kingdom of Heaven or God?

While in seminary, Dr. Don Mauck was gifted to me by the Spirit as a beloved mentor and friend. During my second year, Don asked me to go visit a woman who was actively dying of cancer. She was in her mid-thirties with a loving husband and two young children. I didn't want to go, and for some time I avoided going. But she was dying and there wasn't much time, and Don was insistent. So I went to her hospital room expecting to find someone very depressed, someone for whom I could do nothing, and to then become depressed myself.

She was in bed, attached to a variety of wires and IVs that were delaying her death while monitoring her dying. She was not intubated, and she talked easily. She was one of the most alive people I have ever met. She acknowledged that she was dying and that was that. She spoke of the sadness and the poverty of spirit she felt in dying. She spoke of her husband with deep love. She told me about her wonderful children. She told of her love for horses and her love of life. She told me of how blessed she felt to have had so much amazing love in her few years. She held both being blissful and poor in spirit simultaneously. And the bliss, the happiness, the blessing, held her sadness as a jewel of love. She lived and was dying the paradox of the beatitudes.

In 2002, I was in central Mexico on a study and work project in San Juan Acozac. Our group worked, worshipped, and lived with the people there, most of whom were farmers. They were poor, and many of them were losing their land. Omar was one of those. Through no fault of his own, he had lost his farm and was preparing to leave his family to seek, without documentation, work in Southern California. On our last night, the Evangelica Methodista Iglesia of San Juan Acozac held a fiesta for us. The meat was a pit-roasted lamb. The lamb came from Omar. It was the last animal on his farm. He could have sold it to provide for his family. But he didn't. Instead, he slaughtered his last lamb, dug a pit behind the church, built a fire, let it burn to coals, threw dirt on the coals, wrapped the lamb with some leaves, threw it in the

pit, roasted it, and fed us. Omar was poor, very poor, yet he gave and roasted his last lamb to celebrate us. He felt and offered joy out of his poverty in serving us with lovingkindness.

I asked Omar for a shank bone from the lamb to use during Maundy Thursday dinners as a symbol of the Passover. He gave me one from his fiesta lamb. On my return to El Norte, the shank bone was almost confiscated by the US agricultural customs agent as an illegal item. The explanation of why I had this shank bone in my baggage was confusing to him. How do you explain to a customs agent makaria? Against the rules, he let me keep the bone. I have it in our freezer. It is a prized possession. It reminds me of the Spirit's promise of joy and blessing amid suffering.

Omar was just one member of this remarkable congregation of the happy poor. Their joy and generosity far outshone my own. Turns out, much to the confusion of the rich, that the happy poor are not an anomaly; they are the rule. Research shows that the poor are much more generous than the wealthy. Most of the poor are happy to share their best and last with you. The poor give more of their sparse resources to help others than do the rich of their immense resources. It is a paradox that we who are wealthy find inexplicable and even foolish. However, when surveys of happiness are taken, the poor are far happier than the rich. Such is the kingdom of lovingkindness.

If you have not had the experience of "a peace that passes understanding" or a makaria that transcends the tragedies of life, then I can only tell you that it exists in the generosity of lovingkindness. I have not only repeatedly seen it, but I have also been blessed by it. When Vickie was diagnosed with breast cancer, there was no panic, no sense that we were being swallowed by a dark abyss. We took each test, each surgery, and each treatment one day at a time, leaning into faith, hope, and lovingkindness. Friends, family, and cancer survivors rallied around us and buoyed us with lovingkindness. Joy was ours then and now. Makaria often comes when least expected. I pray blessed joy for you in the hard times. And I pray you may be a blessing for those in hard times, so they may know lovingkindness.

Joy is the unexpected ending, the unanticipated consequence of a life lived in the way of lovingkindness. John Wesley once wrote, "Nothing short of God can satisfy your soul."[11] Lovingkindness satisfies the soul, and our lives become the joyful life we desire and healing for the creation.

In conclusion, I rejoice, am awed, and am grateful that I am not only given the gift of creation but that I am aware of it as lovingkindness. Is it not remarkable that we have eyes to see, ears to hear, minds to wonder, and love to hold? Is it not astounding that we can not only observe creation but reflect on its power and beauty? For the gift of life, I am grateful. I rejoice, am awed, and am grateful for people of lovingkindness in my life. They care for me, forgive me, heal me, and teach me the way of lovingkindness. I rejoice, am awed, and am grateful for the Spirit who comes to me, teaching and healing me to minimize harm, to maximize good, and who leads me to the thin places that I might grow in lovingkindness. I join my quest to be and act in lovingkindness with others, trusting the Spirit to guide and heal us, to transform and perfect us, to use us in and for the well-being of creation.

Remember, I do not profess to know truth but only to offer my interpretation of the shadows on the wall. My life is filled with faith, hope, love, and joy because of lovingkindness. I strive to serve creation with lovingkindness, and I worship the God known to me as lovingkindness.

Shalom and love, Pop.

---

11 John Wesley, "Sermon XII: The Means of Grace," in *John Wesley's Fifty-Three Sermons*, ed. Edward Edward H. Sugden (Nashville, TN: Abingdon Press, 1983), 184.

⌐ APPENDIX 1 ⌐

Other Thoughts

Below are thoughts on random subjects in alphabetical order. They are responses to frequently asked questions in the Amazing Grace classes that inspired this book. The list is not all inclusive. If I am still alive, you can ask me more. If I am dead, I don't know what happens but trust the Spirit to guide you. The best would be for each of us to come to our own understanding of the topics and share.

Believing, Behaving, and Belonging or Belonging, Behaving, and Believing

I recommend Diana Butler Bass's writings to you, particularly *Christianity after Religion: The End of Church and the Birth of a New Spiritual Awakening*, for better understanding of her insights, their history, and their consequences. A fundamental argument of hers is that the earliest church held the pattern of belonging, behaving, and believing: Christians invited people to belong to a community based on loving God and each other. From this belonging grew loving behavior. Out of belonging and loving behavior grew systems of belief.

When the punitive model of salvation took dominance, the order of the pattern flipped to believing, behaving, and belonging. Right belief and right behavior were required before belonging was offered. Butler Bass argues—and I agree—that there is currently a spiritual shift back to belonging, behaving, and believing. This shift, in my opinion, is compatible and supportive of therapeutic salvation. To heal we are invited into a community of lovingkindness. Belonging to this community, we learn and grow in loving behavior. Belonging and behaving in love informs our conversations on what we believe.

Heaven and Hell

John Wesley and I think differently on Heaven and Hell. Wesley held a traditional view. He believed that our thoughts and behavior in this life create a trajectory that lands us either in Heaven or Hell in an afterlife. Heaven is a place of peace and joy. Hell is a place of torment.

I don't know whether there is any kind of life beyond this life. I don't know if such an afterlife would be divided into Heaven and Hell. I don't know what happens when we die. I have spoken with people who have had life-after-death experiences, and I have read the reports of some who have been declared clinically dead, experienced an afterlife, and then been revived. Their stories are fascinating and make me inclined to believe that there is some experience to be had beyond my current biological configuration. If Heaven exists, I would like for it to include Vickie, my children and grandchildren, my parents, my family, my friends, my pets, good food, books, art, mountains, lakes, oceans, sailing, golf, other life-forms, laughter, and beauty. I guess that would make it pretty much like this life with less suffering.

The history of Heaven and Hell can help us understand how we came to a common understanding of these concepts. In the time of Jesus, as today, there were a variety of views. Early Jewish cosmology is one of a three-tiered universe. Heaven is above Earth and Sheol is below Earth. Heaven is a good place where God and the Heavenly Hosts dwell and of which some mystics have experiences. Sheol is a bad place used poetically and prophetically to threaten the unrighteous. "Sheol" is translated into English as "Hell." From the Hebrew scriptures, "Gehenna" is also translated as "Hell." Gehenna is a small, dry valley southwest of Jerusalem. It is infamous as a place of evil, torture, misery, and suffering. No one wants to go or be sent to Gehenna. Sheol is not mentioned in the Christian scriptures. Paul never mentions any form of Hell, though he threatens folks with damnation. The Gospels rarely speak of Hell, but when they do it is of Gehenna and Hades.

Most Jews of Jesus' time didn't consider an afterlife. For them, you lived and then you died. Some thought that in some unknown future there would be the *Day of the Lord* on which a general resurrection of the dead would occur for the righteous. In between now and the general resurrection, there was nothing, neither Heaven nor Hell. Rob Bell, in *Love Wins: At the Heart of Life's Big Questions*, does an excellent job of exploring the question of Hell in Christianity.

We have also inherited concepts of Heaven and Hell from Greek mythology. The Elysian Fields were a wonderful place for those the gods wanted to reward. Hades was a miserable place for those the gods wanted to punish. The gods could be very arbitrary about who went where. Both living and dead could be sent to the Elysian Fields or Hades.

In the Gospels there are also references to the kingdom of Heaven (Matthew) and the kingdom of God (Luke). Both have been understood as an experience of lovingkindness during our earthly life and as a place in an afterlife.

Further, "eternal life" is a translation of the Greek *aionia zoa*. "Aionia" has two understandings in Greek. It can mean "forever," but its most common meaning is "in all times." As noted, "zoa" is a vigorous or healthy life, equivalent to the Hebrew "shalom." "Aionia zoa," translated as "eternal life," is generally understood as an afterlife. The more literal translation is "well-being in all times," the best life possible in this life.

As the first Christians moved from being primarily Jewish to being primarily non-Jewish (Gentile), the concept of Heaven and Hell as places in the afterlife became an amalgam of:

1. The three-tiered cosmos of Heaven, Earth, and Sheol
2. Gehenna as a terrible place to be sent

3. The Jewish resurrection on the Day of the Lord
4. The Greek concept of an afterlife in the Elysian Fields or Hades
5. Gospel references to the kingdom of Heaven or of God
6. Eternal life as an afterlife

It is this synthesis in the Gentile Christian church that gives us the concept of an afterlife that is Heaven for some and Hell for others. The kingdom of Heaven or God was moved from a present experience of love and justice to an afterlife of eternal reward. Hell was moved from being the consequences of failing to love in this life to a place of eternal punishment. Well-being in all times became an eternal afterlife. Later, the punitive model moved the focus from salvation in this life to working out who would go where and why in an afterlife.

Jesus was once asked by the Pharisees when the kingdom of God was coming, and he answered, "The Kingdom of God is not coming with things that can be observed; nor will they say, 'Look, here it is!' or 'There it is!' For in fact, the kingdom of God is among (or within) you."[1]

I believe that the original intent of both Heaven and Hell was to call attention to the consequences of our actions in this life. When I read the Gospels with a first-century Jewish understanding, what Jesus says about the kingdom of Heaven and God is about the experience of lovingkindness in this life. What Jesus says about Gehenna or Hades serves the purpose of warning the unjust. I recognize that I am choosing one interpretation over another. It is also true that both my view of Heaven and Hell as experiences of this life and the more traditional view of Heaven and Hell as experiences in an afterlife can cause an examination of this life. Both views can ask, "Am I living this life in a way to maximize the potential of Heaven and minimize the potential of Hell?" For me, this self-examination is to be done with lovingkindness as the standard. Others have other standards.

I don't believe in Hell as eternal punishment for anyone. I am with Rob Bell on this: love wins! My experience of God is of a lovingkindness

---

1   Luke 17:20–21.

that never gives up on anyone. The Spirit's efforts to heal and reconcile all life remain constant now and forever, in this life and a possible next life. God as the king who damns people to eternal punishment is not the God I experience or in whom I have come to have faith, hope, love, and joy. If there is an afterlife, I don't believe there is one place for the good people and another place for the bad people. If there is an afterlife, it is an afterlife for all life. My guess is that our cooperation or noncooperation with the Spirit in being more loving in this life continues in whatever life may come. But that is just my guess.

Therapeutic salvation is focused on this life and not what happens in a next life. It is in this life that I strive to do no harm, do all the good I can, and cooperate with the healing of the Spirit. I am little concerned with, and rarely think about, a next life, even as my cancer threatens each day. That God is lovingkindness is all I need to understand in this life and any potential next life.

Justice

There are fundamentally two kinds of justice, punitive and reconciling; both are present in the Bible. Punitive justice was an improvement over previous unchecked retribution. Much of the Torah in the Hebrew scriptures is based on the principle of regulated punishment. In Exodus 20:1–17, following the Ten Commandments, is an extended discussion of punitive justice and its limits. Exodus 21:23–25 states, "If any harm follows, then you shall give life for life, eye for eye, tooth for tooth, hand for hand, foot for foot, burn for burn, wound for wound, whipping for whipping."

Punitive salvation is based on the concept that justice is served by punishing the offender. Much of Christianity holds that an unrepentant sinner, in order that God's justice be served, must be punished or God is not truly a just God. I once had an extended conversation with a Reform rabbi friend who thought that there can be no true justice if there is no punishment for crimes against God and humanity. He echoes much of Christian thinking in the punitive model of salvation.

The Bible also contains a concept of compassionate and reconciling justice, which makes the world a place of well-being for everyone. The prophetic tradition is a strong advocate of compassionate and reconciling justice that cares for the poor, the oppressed, and the worldly broken. Mary sings of compassionate and reconciling justice in her Magnificat.[2] Zechariah sees the future of compassionate and reconciling justice when he sings of his baby son, John the Baptist.[3]

When I read the Gospels, I read that Jesus taught compassionate and reconciling justice. In his Sermon on the Mount, an intentional allusion to Moses bringing the Torah from the mountain to the people, Jesus makes a direct reference to the punitive justice of Exodus 21:23–25 when he says, "You have heard that it was said, 'An eye for an eye and a tooth for tooth.' But I say to you, do not resist an evildoer. But if anyone strikes you on the right cheek, turn the other also; and if anyone wants to sue you and take your coat, give your cloak as well, and if anyone forces you to go one mile, go also the second mile. Give to everyone who begs from you, and do not refuse anyone who wants to borrow from you."[4]

There is much to unpack from this quote in the context of Hebrew Scripture and Roman occupation. The bottom line is that Jesus is reinterpreting the meaning of justice within the laws of Moses with the meaning of justice within the prophets, a movement from punishment to compassion and reconciliation.

The Hebrew scriptures Leviticus and Deuteronomy require the community to stone to death those caught in adultery.[5] Jesus reveals the hypocrisy of this punitive requirement when a woman caught in adultery is brought to him for judgment. Jesus says, "Let anyone among you who is without sin [hamartia] be the first to throw a stone at her." When all the accusers leave without casting a stone, and Jesus and the woman are alone, Jesus says to her, "Woman, where are they?

---

2 Luke 1:46–55.

3 Luke 1:67–79.

4 Matthew 5:38–42.

5 Leviticus 17–26; Leviticus 20:10; Deuteronomy 22:22.

Has no one condemned you?" She said, "No one, sir." And Jesus said, "Neither do I condemn you. Go your way, and from now on do not sin again."[6] Jesus refuses to apply the law punitively, instead compassionately offering the woman the return of her life. Jesus moves away from punishment and toward compassion and reconciling justice. He advises that his followers not respond to an attack with "an eye for an eye" but respond in a way that offers the attacker time to reconsider and restore the relationship. He reveals the hypocrisy of anyone punishing another because we all sin, we all fail.

Paul makes the same point when he writes, "For all have sinned and fall short of the glory of God."[7] Compassionate and reconciling justice is not about punishment or retribution. Compassionate and reconciling justice is being willing to forgive as we are forgiven, to be wounded so that another might learn love. It is being willing to sacrifice so that another might have bread and freedom. It is being willing to be crucified so that another might understand the horror of their hate and the healing of lovingkindness.

Of punitive justice, Mahatma Gandhi allegedly said, "An eye for an eye leaves the whole world blind." Gandhi trusted in the transformative power of *satyagrahi*, truth force, for reconciling justice. He believed that being confronted with the truth of suffering can lead a persecutor to their nature of lovingkindness. In essence, turning the other cheek offers to transform the opponent from enemy to ally. This is a process of restoring a right relationship. It is a justice built upon the power of lovingkindness to forgive, reconcile, and heal. It is the process Dr. Martin Luther King Jr. used. It explains, to me, much about Jesus' choice to permit himself to be crucified. Turning the other cheek is a risky process in which the one offering compassion and reconciliation can easily be the victim of fear and anger, of power and greed, and be murdered.

---

6   John 8:1–11.

7   Romans 3:23.

In 1871, the Unitarian minister Theodore Parker spoke these words in opposition to slavery in America: "The arc of the moral universe is long, but it bends toward justice." Dr. Martin Luther King Jr. often repeated Parker's words. God's perfecting of creation into lovingkindness is slow, often too slow for my liking. From a viewpoint high above and removed from the struggle, I see God's persuasive love as ultimately prevailing in life. But on the ground, amid the struggle for justice, I grieve for those who are rejected, brutalized, and killed as the arc too slowly bends.

Naming the Ineffable

There is an ultimate truth, and it has no name. There is a perfect way to be, and none can speak it. Though each knows a part of the path, none knows the way in full. Any name given to ultimate truth, the higher power, the nothing, the force behind all life, limits because it defines what cannot be held in definition. Anyone claiming to know the name of ultimate truth is fooled. Do a quick study or meditate on the Hebrew Scripture's use of YHWH as a reference to the Divine and you will find yourself pulled into a mystical wormhole. It is a wonderful wormhole that leads nowhere and everywhere simultaneously.

Other Religions, Philosophies, and Spiritualities

If a person practices lovingkindness as universal, unconditional, forgiving, reconciling, and healing, a lovingkindness that strives to do no harm, do all the good it can, and offers a way to be transformed by the Spirit into a more loving person and community—then I am for it. If not, then I am against it. It is not my desire that everyone believe as I believe. It is my desire that together we live lovingkindness.

Politics

That we live as a body politic, unless one is an absolute hermit and completely self-sufficient, is simple fact. By this fact, we all participate in politics by action or inaction. What must be discerned is whether action or inaction, at any given moment, is of lovingkindness. Does a thought, word, or action do harm? Does it do all the good it can within the given possibilities? Is it consistent with lovingkindness? Political acts can be voting, boycotting, or protesting. Inaction may be in refusing to participate in violence, refusing/withholding support, or resisting demonizing an opponent. The political goal is for the well-being of all persons and the whole of creation in lovingkindness.

In his daily journal, John Wesley wrote on October 6, 1774, "I met those of our society who had voted in the ensuing election and advised them 1. To vote, without fee or reward for the person they judged most worthy, 2. To speak no evil of the person they voted against, and 3. To take care their spirits were not sharpened against those that voted on the other side."[8] Wise advice, I think.

The Quadrilateral

Albert Outler, in examining the writings of John Wesley, hypothesized that Wesley used four sources for arriving at a conclusion: scripture, tradition, experience, and reason.[9] Scripture, tradition, and reason were standards from the Anglican Church. Wesley added experience. For United Methodists, the combination of the four sources has come to be known as the Quadrilateral.

"Wesley believed that the living core of the Christian faith was revealed in Scripture, illumined by tradition, vivified in personal experience, and confirmed by reason. Scripture [however] is primary, revealing the Word of God so far as it is necessary for our salvation."[10]

---

8 John Wesley, *The Journal of John Wesley*, ntslibrary.com/PDF Books/Wesley_Journal.pdf.

9 Albert Outler, "The Wesleyan Quadrilateral in Wesley," *Wesleyan Theological Journal* 20, no. 1, (Spring 1985), https://wtsociety.com/files/wts_journal/1985-wtj-20-1.pdf.

10 *The Book of Discipline of the United Methodist Church: 2016* (Nashville, TN: The United Methodist Publishing House, 2016), 82.

Scripture

What does scripture have to say about it? Be careful here. The question is not "What am I told, or what have I heard, that scripture says?" Our task is to do the work of studying and praying with scripture personally and corporately.

Tradition

What has the church, the community of faith, thought and done over time? This is research into the roots of a community's thought and action.

Experience

Can it be verified in the experience of the believer and the community?

Reason

Is it reasonable? Is it rational? Will it withstand the critique of others?

(In appendix 3, I use the Quadrilateral to evaluate the United Methodist Church's position on homosexuality.)

Resurrection

Paul, our earliest Christian source, is convinced of the resurrection by a mystical experience that literally knocks him to the ground.[11] Mark's Gospel tells of an empty tomb and alludes to something more.[12] The other three Gospels tell of various kinds of postcrucifixion appearances of Jesus, some similar and others unique to a particular Gospel.[13] The early church seems unanimous that Jesus is raised from the dead

---

11 Acts 9:1–9; Acts 22:1–21; Acts 26:1–23.

12 Mark 16:1-8.

13 Matthew 28; Luke 24; John 20 and 21.

but disparate on the details. For some, it is a spiritual resurrection. For others, there is a resuscitated corpse. And for others, it is both.

Whatever one believes about the resurrection—spiritual, metaphor, physical, or all the above—it leads to the same meaning. After Jesus was dead and the earliest followers, having lost hope, returned to Galilee, something happened that restored their hope so that they preached Jesus resurrected. While Saul was on his way to Damascus to identify and persecute the followers of Jesus, he was struck by the Spirit in such a way that he believed the resurrected Jesus was talking to him. So powerful was the experience that Saul became Paul, the first, and perhaps greatest, Christian evangelist, though he didn't know Jesus before his crucifixion.

There are those who say they too have experienced a resurrected Jesus in their lives. I am at heart a mystic, and I have had experiences that I understand as being of the resurrection. I know that it may be that I delude myself, something we humans are exceptionally good at. And I know my experiences are not evidence for anything other than my foggy and misshapen understanding of my experiences. Whatever the truth of the experiences, the result is that I am repeatedly transformed by these experiences in ways that are beyond the rational or expected. My experiences of the mystery of resurrection, my mystical experiences, have moved me to seek more often to be a person of lovingkindness.

Righteousness

Justice and righteousness are often used interchangeably. If justice is punitive, then righteousness is avoiding punishment by keeping the laws of holiness. But if justice is compassionate and reconciling, then righteousness is doing that which heals the broken and reconciles the estranged. Punitive Christianity generally understands "righteousness" to mean "being right"; that is, keeping the rules. Therapeutic Christianity generally understands righteousness to mean doing right;

that is, acting in lovingkindness. Punitive Christianity generally looks for the right rule and/or statement. Therapeutic Christianity generally seeks to do what offers well-being in a particular situation. Punitive Christianity generally seeks the direction of an external source, usually the Bible used as a rule book and interpreted by an authority. Therapeutic Christianity generally seeks guidance from an authority experienced internally: the Spirit, guided by faith history, those who best live lovingkindness, and their community.

However, I have known folks thoroughly steeped in punitive Christianity who almost always act out of lovingkindness even if it breaks some sacred rule for them. And I have known folks steeped in therapeutic Christianity who have used lovingkindness as a kind of weapon to condemn those with whom they disagree. A friend once told me that in his congregation the pastor encouraged them to help each other spiritually grow by "reproving each other in love." There is good in speaking truth to each other when necessary. But my friend said it had gone so far that when a member of the congregation began, "Sister/brother, I say this to you in love...," you knew you were about to be reproved.

Theodicy

This is a tricky one (aren't they all?). Theodicy is the discussion of the relationship of God and evil. There are three concepts, each assumed to be true, that define the most common discussion of theodicy.

God has power to do whatever God wants to do—God is omnipotent.

God is all good and does no harm—God is omnibenevolent.

Evil exists, causing harm and suffering.

The question of theodicy is then stated in some form of "If God is all powerful and all good, then why is there evil?"

But what if one or more of the assumed concepts is not true? What if God is not all good, is not morally perfect? Carl Jung assumes God is in various stages of moral development, well ahead of us, but still in process. God's relationship with the creation is a part of God's moral maturing. This can certainly be seen in the Bible as God's personality shifts from book to book. Or what if, as the Buddhists argue, there is no such thing as evil and that suffering is a state of the unenlightened non-Buddha mind? If you torture me and I laugh, am I suffering? Process theology generally argues that God is persuasive and not coercive, thus God is limited in ways that permit both moral and natural evil to exist. Take your pick. I choose a combination of Carl Jung, Buddhism, and process theology. But that is just my choice.

Who Killed Jesus?

This is a question from my grandson Trey. He has his reasons, and if you know him, you can ask him. The question has at times been a hot question among Christians because there are those who argue that God sent Jesus to be killed and arranged it so Jesus would be crucified to satisfy God's need for justice through punishment. If this is the case, then God killed Jesus.

The most historical answer, as I understand it, is as follows. Jesus' message was increasingly popular. When Jesus brought his message to Jerusalem, its popularity threatened the power the Jewish religious establishment had over the Jewish populace. To end Jesus' challenge, the religious authorities sought reasons to have a church trial. A religious court, the Sanhedrin, was convened. The Sanhedrin found Jesus guilty of blaspheming against God. In the Jewish Torah, blasphemy is punishable by death.[14]

However, the Jewish religious hierarchy did not have, under Roman law, the authority to execute Jesus. Only Roman civil authority had that power. So the religious authorities took Jesus to the civil authorities, embodied in Pilate, and accused Jesus of plotting against Rome, of insurrection. There were always Jewish zealots seeking to oust Rome

---

14 Leviticus 24:6–10.

from Judea, and so the threat of insurrection was frequently on Pilate's mind. Pilate, as the prefect of Judea, had the power to crucify insurrectionists. Though he seemed to understand that Jesus was not a threat to Rome, Pilate sentenced Jesus to death, doing the dirty work of the Sanhedrin. It appears his primary reason was a political calculation. Maintaining a positive relationship and political peace with the leaders of Judaism was essential for the Pax Romana of Judea.

Jesus supports this history in Luke's Gospel when he cries from the cross, "Abba, forgive them; for they know not what they do."[15] Jesus is holding accountable the people who supported and committed his murder, while also asking God to forgive them. It is not God who murders Jesus, it is religious and civil authorities.

Jesus also says from the cross, "My God, my God why have You abandoned me?"[16] It sounds as if Jesus is accusing God of his death. However, Jesus' cry is the first verse of Psalm 22, which moves from being abandoned by God to praising God, "Offspring shall serve Him; the Lord's name shall be proclaimed to the generation to come; they shall tell of His beneficence to people yet to be born, for He has acted." God has not caused Jesus' death but converts Jesus' death into a beneficial act "to people yet to be born."

That is the basic history. Metaphorically, there is more. When with our voice or by our silence we support religious or political authorities that seek to oppress others, even kill others, that they might maintain their power, we are like the Sanhedrin and Pilate, and we share in their guilt for the death of Jesus.

---

15   Luke 23:34.
16   Matthew 27:46; Mark 15:34.

A Brief History of Salvation

B elow is a brief outline of how the Christian church has understood the purpose and operative function of salvation over time. As the reader can see, there are a variety of interpretations of how the life, death, and resurrection of Jesus may be interpreted as salvific. I wish to demonstrate historically that the perfection, or therapeutic, interpretation of salvation is a millennium earlier than the dominance of the penal, or punitive, interpretation. It is my view that Jesus and the early church should guide our teaching and practice. Hence, the closer our understanding of salvation is to that of Jesus and the earliest church, the more valid it is to guiding us on the way of Jesus.

First- and Second-Century Perfection and Justification

Perfection

This interpretation of salvation was probably the earliest and was dominate through the third century. Its proponents believed that individuals and communities are perfected and thus redeemed through the teachings and moral influence of Jesus. To follow Jesus is to live and love like Jesus. The process of being perfected is amplified by the presence of the resurrected Christ and the Spirit, which are divine aids for the quest to become more Christlike.[1]

Justification

God, through Jesus, battles Satan. Jesus wins the victory by giving his life and then being resurrected by God. With Jesus' victory, the world is reunited with God, resulting in evil losing its power over humanity. This view is dominate from the fourth century until the end of the first millennia of Christianity.[2]

Second and Third Centuries: Ransom Theory

The early church father Origen (184–254) proposed the ransom theory. Humans are captives of evil, of sin. Jesus sets them free from evil by becoming a substitute captive for the world. God sets Jesus free by means of Jesus' resurrection. With Jesus' freedom comes human freedom from sin.

1054: The Christian Church Divided into the Eastern Orthodox and Roman

The Eastern Orthodox Church continued to primarily focus on a therapeutic process of perfection and sanctification, modeling their lives on Jesus and aided in becoming free of sin by the Holy Spirit.

---

1 For the early understanding of what it means to be Christian, see the Didache (Teaching) of the Twelve Apostles. Multiple online translations can be found at http://earlychristianwritings.com/.

2 For an extended discussion see Gustaf Aulén, *Christus Victor: An Historical Study of the Three Main Types of the Idea of the Atonement* (New York: Macmillan, 1979).

Eleventh through Thirteenth Centuries: Debt Satisfaction and Penal Substitution

The Roman Church and then the Protestant church increasingly focused on the debt-satisfaction theory and the penal-substitution theory.

Debt Satisfaction

Proposed primarily by Anselm of Canterbury (1033–1109), Jesus pays the debt we owe God by giving his life for us and we are freed from sin and condemnation. God resurrects Jesus, thus conquering sin and death.

Penal Substitution

Proposed by Thomas Aquinas (1225–1274), this became, over time, the root of punitive salvation. Following his death, Jesus descends into Hell, the eternal prison, as a substitute for us. Though we deserve to be punished, we are set free because of Jesus' substitutionary atonement. God lifts Jesus out of Hell by resurrection and proclaims victory over evil.

Eighteenth Century: John Wesley

John Wesley (1703–1791) emphasized forgiveness, reconciliation, perfection, and sanctification.

Forgiveness and Reconciliation

We are made right with God not by any action of ours, but by God's actions for and in us. Jesus' death testifies to God's willingness to die so we would know the depth of God's love. Jesus' resurrection testifies that even the torture and murder of God does not end God's relationship with us nor God's healing love for us.

Perfection and Sanctification

God is continually offering means by which our thoughts and actions might become more of lovingkindness. Through gratitude, acceptance of forgiveness, and cooperation with the Holy Spirit, we are perfected. As we become more loving, we become better instruments of God's love for all creation, we are sanctified. Of perfecting and sanctifying grace, John Wesley wrote, "God is continually breathing, as it were, upon the soul; and his soul is breathing unto God. Grace is descending into his heart; and prayer and praise ascending to Heaven: and by this intercourse between God and man, this fellowship with the Father and the Son, as by a kind of spiritual respiration, the life of God in the soul is sustained; and the child of God grows up, till he comes to the 'full measure of the stature of Christ.'"[3]

---

3   John Wesley, "Sermon XXXIX: The New Birth," in *John Wesley's Fifty-Three Sermons*, ed. Edward H. Sugden (Nashville, TN: Abingdon Press, 1983), 573.

The Quadrilateral in Use: Homosexuality

C urrently haunting the United Methodist Church (UMC) are questions concerning homosexuality. Is the practice of homosexuality
faithful to Christian teaching? Can a homosexual be a UMC member?
Can a homosexual marry within the UMC? Can a UMC pastor offi-
ciate at a wedding of homosexuals? Can a homosexual be a pastor?
The UMC is governed by the General Conference, which meets every
four years to worship, set budgets, adopt UMC social principles, and
determine polity and policy for the governance of the UMC. United
Methodist polity and policy are written in *The Book of Discipline of
the United Methodist Church*, commonly called *The Book of Discipline*
by United Methodists. I shall be quoting *The Book of Discipline* as the
statement of the UMC's tradition.[1]

What follows is probably more than anyone wants to know. I sometimes catch my wife, children, and grandchildren rolling their eyes
when they ask a simple question and I launch into a dissertation-size
explanation. But this is not a simple question, and I am willing to have
eyes rolled my way.

I limit my discussion to homosexuality and the United Methodist
Church. The United Methodist Church has no policies regarding other

---

1   The most recent edition of *The Book of Discipline of the United Methodist Church* is from the
    2016 General Conference.

members of the LGBTQ+ community.[2] I define homosexuality as "having a preference for same-gender sexual relationships." This is an oversimplified definition, but it is the definition I am using for this focused discussion.

Because I am a pastor, my words and actions belong not only to me, but to a community. I am not just any member of the congregation. I have been called and set aside for ordained, pastoral ministry. My thoughts and actions carry a different weight than those of others in the church. I know I can cause pain in the church community. I do not want to cause pain to my community, be they straight folks or LGBTQ+ folks. Neither do I wish to dodge hard questions because they might cause pain. Hence, I cautiously proceed.

I also know that people can cause their own pain and hurt themselves. Molly Ivins was a newspaper columnist of great wit and wisdom.

She once recounted a story about her late friend, the celebrated Texas civil libertarian John Henry Falk, who, as a boy of six, went with his seven-year-old friend, Boots Cooper, to rid the family henhouse of a harmless chicken snake. From its high perch, the snake frightened the two boys, who fought each other in their hurry to exit the henhouse. When Falk's mother reminded the boys that chicken snakes are not dangerous, Boots Cooper responded, "Yes, ma'am, but some things will scare you so bad, you'll hurt yourself."[3]

Homosexuality seems to be for us one of those things that can scare us so badly we hurt ourselves. I pray that as a community we do not react to homosexuality or my thoughts as the two boys reacted to the chicken snake. I hope to move gently about the chicken house for the sake of the door, the chickens, the snake, and me.

---

2   I am aware that the acronym LGBTQ+ is not complete for some folks, that there are variants that are better for others, and that its intended identification of a particular community is inadequate. I pray those who would express this differently will forgive me and understand my choice is the best I can offer as we move toward the necessary new language. Sexuality is a lot more complicated than any label can capture.

3   This story has been often repeated. I have used the version from Berkeley.edu, "Molly Ivins Said *That?*," https://www.berkeley.edu/news/berkeleyan/2004/10/14_ivins.shtml.

I am grateful to the book *Is the Homosexual My Neighbor?*[4] because it was a helpful early resource as I studied the scriptures that have been rightly or wrongly applied to homosexuality. A recently discovered resource is *Walking the Bridgeless Canyon*,[5] which covers not only scripture, but also the history of oppression in culture, theology, politics, psychology, psychotherapy, and churches. As a bonus, there is an excellent chapter on biology and genetics.

United Methodists are encouraged by *The Book of Discipline* to consider questions of faith and action in the contexts of scripture, tradition, experience, and reason, generally called by United Methodists the Quadrilateral.[6] The following discussion will follow that format. I conclude that the Bible does not comment on homosexuality, that the United Methodist tradition is confusing and conflicted, that reason concludes homosexuality is not a choice and but a biological given, and that my experience of homosexual persons is that they are complex human beings seeking to love and be loved.

Scripture

It is proposed by some that the Bible clearly stands opposed to homosexuality; if the Bible is against homosexuality, then so is God; and if God is against homosexuality, then we should also be against it. Jesus says nothing about homosexuality. The frequently quoted passages to support the Bible's opposition to homosexuality are the destruction of Sodom and Gomorrah,[7] portions of Israel's Holiness Code,[8] Paul's let-

---

4   Letha Dawson Scanzoni and Virginia Ramey Mollenkott, *Is the Homosexual My Neighbor?*, (New York: Harper and Row, 1978, revised and updated in 1994).

5   Kathy Baldock, *Walking the Bridgeless Canyon* (Reno, NV: Canyonwalker Press, 2014).

6   *The United Methodist Book of Discipline*, Our Theological Task, 105 (The United Methodist Publishing House, 2016).

7   Genesis 19.

8   Leviticus 18:22, 20:13.

ter to the churches in Corinth and Rome,[9] and verses in the pseudo Pauline letter to Timothy.[10]

Genesis 19

Two angels come to town and Lot offers the hospitality of his home. A town mob demands to have "intercourse" or "come to know" the angels. There is ambiguity in the Hebrew text as to whether sexual or conversational intercourse is meant. The mob threatens Lot and his family. Lot offers his daughters to the mob as a substitute for the angels. The mob refuses the daughters and tries to break into Lot's house, but the angels prevent them. Then the angels announce that they will destroy the city, and Lot should take his family and leave. The passage does not explain the angels' decision to destroy Sodom and Gomorrah.

Most scholars believe that Sodom and Gomorrah are destroyed because of Sodom's inhospitable and abusive acts in contrast to Lot's generous hospitality. Jesus affirms this understanding when he uses Sodom as an example of what will happen to the inhospitable.[11] I stand with Jesus' understanding of the destruction of Sodom and Gomorrah. It is about inhospitality, not homosexuality.

Leviticus 18:22 and 20:13

Both passages call "a man lying with a man as if with a woman" an abomination. Leviticus 20:13 requires those engaged in such behavior be put to death. Both passages certainly seem to be condemning male homosexual behavior. Both passages are a part of the Hebrew Scripture's Holiness Code. The Code is a list on how to be clean, holy, before God and the circumstances that make one unclean before God.

The Holiness Code is a small portion of the Torah. The standard count of the number of Torah laws is 613. Mostly only ultraorthodox Jews attempt to keep the entire Torah, and they have all kinds of special

---

9   1 Corinthians 6:9; Romans 1:26–27.

10 1 Timothy 1:10.

11 Luke 10:10–12.

interpretations, conditions, and exceptions. Most of us ignore most of the Torah. For instance, we ignore the double "abomination" of eating a ham and cheese sandwich. Pork is a no-no,[12] and cheese as dairy is not to be combined with meat.[13] More seriously, the list includes permission to enslave others from neighboring nations and to sell a daughter into slavery. It forbids the eating of meat with blood in it and declares that a woman menstruating is unclean and all who have contact with her or any object she may have touched are made unclean before God. What is unclean is an "abomination."

Regarding Leviticus 18:22 and 20:13, some scholars have argued that both are a reference to male cult prostitutes who were employed for same-sex sexual acts during religious rituals. Others have pointed to the practice of powerful men having boys for sex slaves. The issue for these scholars is the use of cult prostitutes or sex slaves; it is not sexual preference. I agree that cult prostitution and sex slaves are abominations before God. But this is not homosexuality as we now know it, where two men consensually have sex.

Some scholars disagree and argue that this passage is indeed about male homosexuality. If these scholars are correct, and if homosexuality is understood in these passages to in fact be an "abomination" to God, then I willfully break this part of the Holiness Code by refusing to condemn and kill male homosexuals.

This is not the only rule of the Torah I willfully ignore or refuse. I confess that I sometimes eat ham with cheese, steaks medium to rare, lobster, shrimp, and crab. If you tell me that Paul and Peter agreed to end the prohibitions on food, then I ask why we don't end it on homosexuality? Or, stated inversely, why do we choose to keep some laws of the Torah and not others? Why does homosexuality give rise to such heated discussions when we laugh at the ban on wearing mixed fibers?[14] I will not enslave anyone even if they are from a neighboring

---

12 Deuteronomy 14:8.

13 This is the rabbinic interpretation of Exodus 23:19, Exodus 34:26, and Deuteronomy 14:21, which state that it is forbidden to "boil a (goat) kid in its mother's milk."

14 Leviticus 19:19.

country, and even though it may be okay with God. I did not find my wife, nor do I find any woman, unclean and defiling while menstruating, nor did I send my wife to the red tent and require of her a ritual bath. Just as I disagree with the Torah on slavery, dairy, meat, shellfish, and menstruation, I also disagree with its supposed condemnation of male homosexuality. In these ways and more, I am willfully and unrepentantly in violation of some of the Torah.[15] I question why we choose to see some of Moses' laws as necessary, such as "Thou shalt not kill," and others, such as permission to enslave anyone, as horrid, and yet others, such as eating crab or ham, as archaic and insignificant.

If these passages are about temple prostitution or sex slaves, then they are not about homosexuality. If they are about homosexuality, then I ask why the prohibition of male-to-male sexual relationships should not be ignored in the same manner that we ignore the prohibition to eat ham or lobster, resisted as we resist enslaving anyone, and condemned in the same way some name the Torah's treatment of menstruating women as misogyny.

1 Corinthians 6:9

In his first letter to the church in Corinth, Paul asks the Corinthians, "Do you not know that the unrighteous will not inherit the kingdom of God?" He then goes on to give examples of the "unrighteous." *Arsenokoitos* and *malakos* are two of the Greek words in the list. They have been translated by some to be "homosexual" and "effeminate." We will spend a little time with each.

The Abridged Liddell and Scott Greek-English Lexicon translates "arsenokoitos" as "one guilty of unnatural offenses." The unabridged version translates it as "sodomite." "Arsenokoites" wasn't translated as "homosexual" until the 1947 edition of the *Revised Standard Version* (*RSV*) of the Bible. Subsequent versions of the *RSV* (*RSV* Second Edition, 1971 and the *New Revised Standard Version*, 1990) have not

---

15   For a longer but not all-inclusive list of Torah I don't keep, see appendix 4.

made this same translation but use the more generalized term "sodomite" for sexual immorality.

"Arsenokoites" is a compound word of "male" and "bed." Paul, as best we know, was the first in the whole of Greek language to use "arsenokoitos" as a compound word. The second use is by the author of 1 Timothy, who is copying Paul. Some suggest Paul may have coined it as a reference to Leviticus 20:13. Philo, a Jewish theologian in Alexandria during the time of Paul and Jesus, understood a Greek translation of the Hebrew scriptures use of *arsenos koitev* (note that it is two words) in Leviticus 20:13 as a reference to temple or cult prostitution.[16]

The bottom line is we can only guess what "arsenokoites" means. Those guesses have included male prostitutes with female customers, cult prostitution, older males who bed young boys, and sexual acts between males. I repeat, we don't know what "arsenokoites" means.

Malakos is equally frustrating to translate.[17] It is generally translated as "soft" or "things soft to the touch." The translation of "malakos" as "effeminate" may have originated in the cultural characterization of women as morally weak or soft. Matthew 11:18 and Luke 7:25 use "malakos" to indicate an undesirable moral flexibility, a moral softness. *The Theological Dictionary of the New Testament (IV, 1091)* lists "malakos" as a synonym of *nosos*, a sickness related to sin. Which sin and which sickness is not specified. The 1970 *New English Bible* translates "malakos" as "adultery." The 1971 *RSV* says "adulterers." The 1973 *RSV* uses "adulterers." The 1990 *NRSV* translates "malakos" as "male prostitutes." When Paul includes "malakos" in a list of the "unrighteous," it is unclear to translators what is he talking about.

---

16 Philo, *The Special Laws*, III, VII, 40–42, circa 35 CE. Two online articles on *arsenokoites* that I found especially helpful are Sean Isler's "History of *Arsenokoites*," *Bible Abuse Directed at Homosexuals*, January 26, 2009, https://www.stopbibleabuse.org/biblical-references/paul/arsenokoites.html; and Shylo Rosborough's "Arsenokoitai," Robertson-Wesley United Church, March 20, 2020, https://www.rwuc.org/2020/03/20/arsenokoitai/.

17 A good online discussion that is much more complete can be found at stopbibleabuse.org under "Malakos—Bible Abuse Directed at Homosexuals."

Romans 1:26–27

In his letter to the church in Rome, Paul groups "unnatural relations" with lust, lying, gossip, and other ways of acting that are displeasing to God. Paul does not use a word for homosexuals.[18] Some translators and interpreters have posited that what Paul calls "unnatural relations" are homosexual acts. If we assume, a priori, that Paul is referring to a sexual relationship and that any same-sex sexual act is an "unnatural relationship," then the passage can be a read as a condemnation of homosexuality.

However, if a person's natural sexual preference is same-gender, then a homosexual act is natural, according to their nature, and a heterosexual act would be unnatural, against their nature. This passage does not address the issue of persons whose natural sexual orientation is same-gender.[19] In fact, it seems that Paul knows nothing or is not commenting about persons who are by nature homosexual.

1 Timothy 1:9–10

In order for homosexuality to be among the list in this passage, "arsenokoites" must be translated as "homosexual." I am intentionally redundant when I say we don't know what Paul, or the pseudo-Paul writing to Timothy, meant by "arsenokoites." The actions listed by 1 Timothy 1:9–10 are translated variously by different versions of the Bible. For example, in the *RSV*, *andrapodistais* is both "kidnapper" (1971) and "slave trader" (1990). Other items in the list also show a great diversity of translations. The stated purpose is to exemplify what is lawless and disobedient, ungodly and sinful, unholy and profane. Every item in the list is one in which there is an abuser and an abused, or in which abuse is assumed; the murdering child and the murdered

---

18 In fact, Biblical Greek has no word for homosexual and homosexuality unless *arsenokoites* is translated as homosexual and we have already seen the problem with that. The category of "having a preference for same gender sexual relationships" is a modern construct.

19 Under the section on reason, I will discuss whether there is clear evidence that there are persons who are naturally, or by birth, homosexual.

parent, murders and those they murder in general, immoral persons in general, arsenokoites (?) kidnapper and kidnapped. Each listed item is an example of one person abusing another. What 1 Timothy is saying is "abusing another person is lawless, disobedient, ungodly, sinful, unholy and profane." I totally agree.

My reading of the Bible suggests that for persons who are homosexual, the Bible, like Jesus, says nothing. Homosexuality as an innate sexual preference for sexual relations with same-gender persons is not discussed in the Bible.

Tradition

United Methodists have struggled long and hard with the issues surrounding human sexuality, and in particular, homosexuality. Below is a review of the current United Methodist tradition as printed in *The Book of Discipline* regarding homosexuality. *The Book of Discipline* is divided into paragraphs, and I have listed the relevant paragraph numbers.

The Book of Discipline contains the Social Principles of the United Methodist Church and ¶ 161 is in that section.

> ¶ 161: Language of a derogatory nature (with regard to race, nationality, ethnic background, gender, sexuality, and physical differences) does not reflect value for one another and contradicts the gospel of Jesus Christ.

Paragraph 161 continues and specifically speaks about human sexuality:

> ¶ 161F: We affirm that sexuality is God's good gift to all persons. We call everyone to responsible stewardship of this sacred gift... Although all persons are sexual beings whether or not they are married, sexual relations are affirmed only with the covenant of monogamous, heterosexual marriage.
>
> We deplore all forms of the commercialization, abuse, and exploitation of sex. We call for strict global enforcement

of laws prohibiting the sexual exploitation of children and for adequate protection, guidance, and counseling for abused children. All persons, regardless of age, gender, marital status, or sexual orientation, are entitled to have their human and civil rights ensured and to be protected against violence. The Church should support the family in providing age-appropriate education regarding sexuality to children, youth, and adults.

We affirm that all persons are individuals of sacred worth, created in the image of God. All persons need the ministry of the Church in their struggles for human fulfillment, as well as the spiritual and emotional care of a fellowship that enables reconciling relationships with God, with others, and with self. The United Methodist Church does not condone the practice of homosexuality and considers this practice incompatible with Christian teaching. We affirm that God's grace is available to all. We will seek to live together in Christian community, welcoming, forgiving, and loving one another, as Christ has loved and accepted us. We implore families and churches not to reject or condemn lesbian and gay members and friends. We commit ourselves to be in ministry for and with all persons.

This a remarkable statement of the "sacred worth" of all persons. But marriage is only for heterosexuals. Inserted and inconsistent with what precedes and what follows is, "The United Methodist Church does not condone the practice of homosexuality and considers this practice incompatible with Christian teaching." On one hand, we say, "God's grace is available to all" and ask each other "not to reject or condemn lesbian and gay members or friends." But on the other hand, we declare that the practice of homosexuality is "incompatible with Christian teaching." We deplore language that is derogatory, but what could be more derogatory than to name someone's sexual life "incompatible with Christian teaching"? Note that we do not say that homosexuality is incompatible with scripture, only that it is incompatible with what we teach. Nor do we say that homosexuals as persons are judged to be outside of grace or salvation; they are to be included. Further, we say that it is not homosexuality that is "incompatible with Christian teaching," but the practice of homosexuality. Thus, it is okay to be homosexual if it is not practiced. It is okay to have homosexual desires if you don't act on those desires. These are conflicted messages and indicate the conflict of our tradition.

> ¶ 304.3: The practice of homosexuality is incompatible with Christian teaching. Therefore, self-avowed practicing homosexuals are not to be certified as candidates, ordained as ministers, or appointed to serve in the United Methodist Church.

A second time *The Book of Discipline* states the tradition that the practice of homosexuality is incompatible with Christian teaching. But tradition is not scripture; it is what we have taught and how we have behaved over time. Tradition is shaped by culture, which may be of prejudice, ignorance, and malice. Tradition must be altered when it is used to oppress others. The United Methodist Church has changed its tradition in the cases of slavery, racism, and sexism. The United Methodist Church now has candidates, ordinands, and Elders who are people of color and who are women. Not that long ago both were excluded from being UMC pastors by the tradition encoded in *The Book of Discipline.*

The Judicial Council, the Supreme Court of the United Methodist Church, has decided that the words "self-avowed practicing homosexuals" mean just what they say. Because a clergy person says they are homosexual is not sufficient ground to revoke or deny their credentials (Judicial Council decisions 542 and 544). Homosexuals must be both self-avowed homosexuals and practicing homosexuals. Again, our tradition says that it is the practice of homosexuality that is undesirable, not the fact of being homosexual. This is confusing. If it is acceptable to be a homosexual, then why is it not acceptable to practice what you are? Couldn't someone argue that they have practiced homosexuality, but they are not actually homosexual and therefore can be ordained and appointed as a pastor?

> ¶ 341.6: Ceremonies that celebrate homosexual unions shall not be conducted by our ministers and shall not be conducted in our churches.

So, though we argue the homosexual's right to behave legally and socially as married partners, we refuse to let our clergy bless this marriage or for our buildings to be used for such a blessing. That is, though we argue for homosexuals' legal rights as if they are a married couple, their marriage cannot be blessed by UMC pastors. Again, our tradition is conflicted and even oppressive. Either committed homosexual relationships are like marriages and should be treated as such legally and spiritually, or they are not like marriages and must be denied not only our blessing but our support in any way.

> ¶ 613: The [Conference Council on Finance and Administration] shall have authority and responsibility to...ensure that no annual conference board, agency, committee, commission, or council shall give United Methodist funds to any gay caucus or group, or otherwise use such funds to promote the acceptance of homosexuality or violate the expressed commitment of The UMC "not to reject or condemn lesbian and gay members and friends" (¶ 161F).
>
> ¶ 806.9: [The General Council on Finance and Administration] shall be responsible for ensuring that no board, agency, committee, commission, or council shall give United Methodist funds to any gay caucus or group, or otherwise use such funds to promote the acceptance of homosexuality or violate the expressed commitment of The United Methodist Church "not to reject or condemn lesbian and gay members and friends" (¶ 161F)

It is so important that no agency of the UMC give funds to support the acceptance of homosexuality that almost the exact wording is used for a variety of UMC agencies. Although we are directed by *The Book of Discipline* to give vocal support to gay rights, we are forbidden to give financial support. However, when a pastor or congregation, who both receive considerable financial support from the UMC, offers support to homosexual persons and encourages support of homosexual persons, as *The Book of Discipline* encourages, then that pastor or congregation is in violation of ¶613 and ¶806.9. This is yet another conflicted part of our tradition.

The confusion continues in ¶2702(b), which lists chargeable offenses for clergy:

> ¶ 2702: 1. A bishop, clergy member of an annual conference (¶ 370), local pastor, clergy on honorable or administrative location, or diaconal minister may be tried when charged (subject to the statute of limitations in ¶ 2702.4) with one or more of the following offenses: (a) immorality including but not limited to, not being celibate in singleness or not faithful in a heterosexual marriage; (b) practices declared by The United Methodist Church to be incompatible with Christian teachings including but not limited to: being a self-avowed practicing homosexual; or conducting ceremonies which celebrate homosexual unions; or performing same-sex wedding ceremonies; (c) crime; (d) disobedience to the order and discipline of The United Methodist Church; (e) dissemination of doctrines contrary to the established standards of doctrine of The United Methodist Church; (f) relationships and/or behavior that undermines the ministry of another pastor; (g) child abuse; (h) sexual abuse; i) sexual misconduct including the use or possession of pornography; (j) harassment, including, but not limited to racial and/or sexual harassment; (k) racial or gender discrimination; or (l) fiscal malfeasance.

Being a self-avowed practicing homosexual, conducting ceremonies that celebrate homosexual unions, or performing same-sex wedding ceremonies are listed with all kinds of crimes for which clergy can be brought to a church trial by any member of the United Methodist Church. This places homosexuality on the same level as child abuse, when earlier we are instructed not to say derogatory words about homosexuals.

There are also chargeable offenses for laity.

> ¶ 2702.3: A lay member of a local church may be charged with the following offenses, and, if so, may choose a trial: (a) immorality; (b) crime; (c) disobedience to the Order and Discipline of The United Methodist Church; (d) dissemination of doctrines contrary to the established standards of doctrine of The United Methodist Church; (e) racial harassment; (f) sex abuse; (g) sexual misconduct; (h) sexual harassment; or (i) child abuse.

These chargeable offenses do not include anything about homosexuality. So, clergy can be charged, go to trial, and lose their credentials because they are self-avowed practicing homosexuals, or because they bless or perform same-sex weddings, but it is okay if you are not clergy to bless same-sex weddings (except it is still "incompatible with Christian teaching"). Our denomination's position is again confusing and conflicted.

Our tradition is formed in our conversations with each other and evolves over time. Heated and intense discussions about homosexuality have happened at past United Methodist conferences and will happen again at upcoming conferences for we remain divided over homosexuality. Votes will be taken, and margins will be slight as we continue to search for what we believe God would have us say and do about persons of same-gender preference in their sexual orientation. The discussions and votes at the last General Conference, and the obvious conflicts within our written tradition, indicate that United

Methodists are very much divided around the issue of homosexuality and homosexual persons. The confusion of the UMC tradition reflects its struggling conflict and division.

Experience

Each of us has our own experience. In 1972 Charlie became, as far as I know, my first gay friend. Before Charlie, sexual preference was not a question I had considered. After Charlie and others, it is a question I refuse to ignore. I am sure that I was acquainted with homosexuals prior to seminary but I didn't know they were homosexual. Charlie loved drama, as I do. He was a gifted actor with a wonderful singing voice. On stage he lifted me to his level of performance. He was an outstanding student at the Methodist Theological School in Ohio. Charlie was compassionate, known for his generous and kind ways, particularly with the brokenhearted or persecuted. Charlie was ordained and successfully pastored a United Methodist Church. When Charlie was diagnosed with AIDS, he told his congregation that he was ill and that he was homosexual. Then he told us, his friends, the news of his illness and his sexual orientation. Charlie's congregation kept him as their pastor until he died because they loved him. Almost all his friends kept him as a friend because we loved him.

My experience teaches me that except for sexual orientation, homosexual persons are people like me. They need to love and be loved. They need to know that their lives have value for our world. They make the same mistakes I do and have many of the same failings I possess. My experience teaches me that I cannot tell a homosexual from a heterosexual unless I am told. My experience teaches me that homosexual persons eat with me, go to the movies with me, watch basketball with me, pay taxes with me, work with me, pray with me, worship with me, and live life in much the same way I do. My experience teaches me that homosexual persons are my neighbor, and scripture and tradition clearly teach me to love my neighbor.

Reason

Various genetic, physiological, and psychological studies have produced increasingly clear results. When in 1995 I began my intentional research of the science in this area, the scientific results were suggestive but inconclusive. Current research into genetics and the chemistry of the brain have convinced most scientists, physicians, and psychologists that sexual preference is innate to the individual person's biochemical and genetic composition.

Our sexuality is not as simple as "he or she loves her or him." If my physiology and gender identification align and I am attracted to persons of the opposite gender, then I am heterosexual. However, there are many possible variations that may be present in personal physiology, biochemistry, genetic composition, and mental construct. These variations are not unique to humans but are also found in other mammals. Our gender identification may not match the gender we are assigned at birth. We may then decide to align our bodies with our gender identification. And it may be that as a transgender female we are sexually attracted to women, so we are homosexual. But we could also be heterosexual, bisexual, or asexual. Intersex people face other complicated questions and decisions.

Kathy Baldock's *Walking the Bridgeless Canyon* has a great summary of the science and references to the relevant research as of 2014. Since then, even more information has underlined the point that our physiology, gender identification, and sexual preference are independent of each other, exist on continuums, and are not choices we make. We are born with variations in all three aspects of being sexual.

To most heterosexuals, homosexuality seems unnatural and undesirable. If homosexuality seemed natural and desirable to me, then I would be homosexual. It is reasonable to assume that if desire leads us in one direction, then the opposite direction would be undesirable, unnatural to us, and perhaps even feel threatening. I resist reacting to our differences with fear. The diversity of sexuality (or race, or talent, or anything else in God's great diversity) is a gift of God, and a great many of us are remarkable not for how we are alike, but for how our differences enhance and enrich our community.

The medical and psychiatric community tell us that homosexuality is not an illness; that for a homosexual, the acceptance of their sexual preference is a part of being a healthy individual. The research is sufficient for me, and for the American Medical Association and for the American Psychological Association, to conclude that a reasonable mind will regard gender identification and sexual preference as almost always biologically determined characteristics and not choices.

My Conclusions

Scripture does not speak of persons whose sexual preference is same gender. It is obvious to even the casual observer that UMC tradition is confused and conflicted regarding homosexuality. I experience homosexual people as mostly wonderful people in the same way I experience most people as wonderful. Reason through scientific research tells us that the relationship between physiology, gender identity, and sexual preference occurs on continuums, in a variety of combinations, and is not a choice but is a part of one's genetic and biochemical makeup.

Our sexuality is so important to the deepest foundations of our identity that our conversations around sexuality are emotionally supercharged. For many of us, to simply have the subject raised is frightening. And like the two boys escaping the chicken house, "some things will scare you so bad, you'll hurt yourself." I pray that we will not be hurt by our fear but be lifted to compassion by God's grace. I pray that we regard Jesus' statement that the most important law of God is in two parts: "to love God with all our heart, mind, soul, and strength" and "to love our neighbor as ourselves." It is this commandment by which we are called to apply how we live our lives in the world before we make any other judgment or take any action. If I am to err in my words or by my actions to my homosexual neighbor, then I pray I err on the side of lovingkindness and justice, calling each my friend, my brother and sister in Christ, even my esteemed colleague.

My Actions

The United Methodist Church has a long history of being firmly and publicly supportive of full human rights for homosexuals. It has been for many of us an issue of ending oppression and establishing justice. For many years I have been active and vocal in support of the LGBTQ+ community and their rights, both legal and spiritual. I helped form one of the earliest chapters of Parents and Friends of Lesbians and Gays (PFLAG) in Montana. I have organized and led classes to discuss human sexuality. Several lesbian, gay, and transgender people have been leaders, members, or regular attendees of congregations I served. I have intentionally had members of the LGBTQ+ community assist, lead, sing, pray, and preach in worship. I have testified at state and church legislative hearings, attended public rallies, and marched in Pride events. I have a grandson who is transgender and identifies as queer. Never have I tried to hide or minimize my commitment to make the church a safe, inclusive, and just place for all of God's children. I will continue to be an advocate for my LGBTQ+ family.

APPENDIX 4

Some Torah I Don't Keep

When I first wrote this appendix, I inserted sarcastic and snarky remarks about each law. Later, I repented and now offer a list of laws from the Bible for the reader to decide if each is a law they keep, and think must be kept, to please God. However, for number ten I retained my comments because number ten is personal.

Most of us treat the Torah as if there are greater and lesser abominations. Eating shellfish isn't so bad, but selling a daughter into slavery is very bad. I don't think the Bible supports such a hierarchical understanding of abominations.

1. Exodus 21:7 permits me to sell my daughter into slavery.
2. Exodus 35:2 clearly states I should put to death those who work on the Sabbath (Friday sundown to Saturday sundown).
3. Leviticus 11:6–8 indicates that touching the skin of a dead pig makes me unclean.
4. Leviticus 11:10–11 forbids eating shellfish.
5. Leviticus 15:19–24 says I am allowed no contact with a woman while she is in her time of menstrual uncleanliness.
6. Leviticus 19:19 says planting two different crops in the same field or wearing a garment made of two different materials is an abomination.
7. Leviticus 19:27 tells me to not trim my hair, including the hair around the temples, nor trim my beard.
8. Leviticus 19:28 says I may not have any tattoos.

9. Leviticus 20:14 tells me to burn to death any man who sleeps both with his wife and her mother.

10. Leviticus 21:16–20 tells me no one who has a blemish—such as being blind or lame; having a mutilated face, a too-long limb, a broken foot or hand; being hunchback or a little person; having an itching disease, scabs, or crushed testicles—may approach God. I have atopic dermatitis, which causes itching. I am nearsighted and wear glasses. Does a vasectomy count as crushed testicles? The hormone therapy I am receiving for metastasized prostate cancer is also known as medical castration. Does this count?

11. Leviticus 24:10–16 tells me to organize the community to stone to death anyone who is a blasphemer.

12. Leviticus 25:44 states that I may possess slaves, both male and female, provided they are from neighboring nations.

Suggested Reading

David Adam

Church Forward to Freedom: From Exodus to Easter

The Eye of the Eagle: Meditations on the Hymn "Be Thou My Vision"

Stanley Ayling

John Wesley

Marcus Borg

The God We Never Knew: Beyond Dogmatic Religion to a More Authentic Contemporary Faith

Jesus: A New Vision

Jesus: Uncovering the Life, Teachings, and Relevance of a Religious Revolutionary

Reading the Bible Again for the First Time

Diana Butler Bass

Christianity after Religion

Christianity for the Rest of Us

A People's History of Christianity

Paul W. Chilcote, ed.

The Wesleyan Tradition: A Paradigm for Renewal

John Cobb

Becoming a Thinking Christian

Grace and Responsibility: A Wesleyan Theology for Today

Jesus' Abba: The God who Has Not Failed

Praying for Jennifer: An Exploration of Intercessory Prayer in Story Form

Richard Foster
Celebration of Discipline: The Path to Spiritual Growth

Matthew Fox
Original Blessing

Edward Goldsmith
The Way: An Ecological World-View

Thich Nhat Hahn
Miracle of Mindfulness: An Introduction to the Practice of Meditation
Peace Is Every Step: The Path of Mindfulness in Everyday Life

Theodore W. Jennings Jr.
Good News to the Poor: John Wesley's Evangelical Economics

Randy Maddox
Responsible Grace: John Wesley's Practical Theology

Michael Mitton
Restoring the Woven Cord: Strands of Celtic Christianity for the Church Today

Albert Outler
Evangelism in the Wesleyan Spirit

Edward Sugden, ed.
John Wesley's Fifty-Three Sermons

Evelyn Underhill
Mysticism: A Study of the Nature and Development of Man's Spiritual Consciousness
Practical Mysticism

Acknowledgments

What I write and trust is from a lifetime of teachers, mentors, writers, parishioners, friends, family, strangers, and a few enemies. I love the work of academia, but more important to me are those who have loved me. A host of people, creatures, views, and visions have shaped me and continue to work their healing within me. Being married and being a parent and grandparent have had the utmost influence on who I am becoming. In my family life I am often discovered and healed by living the Spirit of God. I thank you all.

I am particularly indebted to the biblical, philosophical, historical, and theological works of John Cobb, Randy Maddox, Paul Chilcote, Albert Outler, Alfred North Whitehead, E. Stanley Jones, Elisabeth Schussler Fiorenza, Robert Tannehill, Burton Mack, Karl Barth, Emil Brunner, Martin Buber, Evelyn Underhill, Paul Tillich, Elaine Pagels, Matthew Fox, Dee Eck, John Dominic Crossan, Marcus Borg, Diana Butler Bass, and Abraham Heschel. I am strongly influenced by the work of the Jesus Seminar of The Society of Biblical Literature on the historical Jesus. The Depth Psychology of Carl Jung along with the psychologists Viktor Frankl, William Glasser, and Kazimierz Dabrowski are foundational. In science, Paul Davies writing on God and physics and Edward Goldsmith on ecology have been of significant value. The novelists Nikos Kazantzakis, Irving Stone, and Ursula Le Guin are favorites that shape and reshape me. The lives and teachings of Jesus, Albert Schweitzer, Buddha of the Mahayana tradition, and Lao Tzu continue to guide my living.

I thank those who have read the various drafts and helped me make improvements. Joni Rodgers is a friend who gave good advice and directed me to The Reading List with Lindsey Alexander and Salvatore Borriello. Lindsey, Sal, and their team assisted me in vastly improving the quality of the writing and presentation. My friends Mark Scow and Dennis Lone also read and gave excellent advice on improvements.

One of my father's favorite quotes is most often attributed to Sir Isaac Newton, though the concept can be dated to the twelfth-century French philosopher Bernard of Chartres: "If I have seen farther than others, it is by standing upon the shoulders of giants." I am not aware that I have seen farther than others, but I am quite aware of standing on the shoulders of giants, and I have tried to give credit where credit is due. Nothing I say is original. Everything I say is begged, borrowed, or stolen from someone wiser than me. I thank them, and I apologize for any misstatement or abuse of their wisdom.

About David Orendorff

David Orendorff is a retired United Methodist pastor who served congregations in Wyoming, Ohio, California, Montana, and Washington. He now resides in Woodinville, Washington, with his wife, Vickie, and is blessed to live near all his children and grandchildren. He continues to occasionally preach, teach, consult, and mentor.

About Trey Schaaf

While in his teens, Trey Schaaf became a professional artist, receiving commissions and payments for his work. Because his dominant hand and wrist were damaged by overuse in his efforts to be self-supportive, Trey used his nondominant left hand for the art of this book. Trey identifies himself as transmasculine queer. He currently attends The Evergreen State College in Olympia, Washington. He aspires to be an art teacher for secondary students. He hopes to offer a safe classroom of lovingkindness for his students as did the teachers who supported and cared for him through his years growing up.

You can view the power of Trey's art and support him by visiting tothesolarium.threadless.com/collections/the-book-of-loving-kindness. There you will find the art in this book and more of his creativity.

Made in the USA
Las Vegas, NV
11 November 2022

59181924R00090